THE HUMAN TOUCH
in the art of ballet

THE HUMAN TOUCH

in the art of ballet

by Shelagh McKenna

Unicorn Publishing
Sooke, Canada
2020

FOREWORD

Movement is a mode of expression for which no substitute exists. Just as there is no possibility of fully translating a poem from one language to another, there is no alternative manner in which to create the effect of a dance. A work of art is inseparable from its meaning, which can be found only in sound, story, image or motion itself.

Consequently, any attempt to relate a ballet would be as futile as an attempt to dance a novel. The following articles demonstrate no such intention on my part. Their subject happens to be the impure element in some of my favourite ballets, which can be described in words precisely because it is impure. Observing many Balanchine ballets, for example, an admirer seeking converts must resort to pulling out a musical score or a choreology of the work to be appreciated, or else can do no more than expose the audience to repeated performances. And if the response is persistent lack of appreciation, nothing can be done. You cannot make other people care that Balanchine brought the ballet stage to life when he divided the corps de ballet into factions. And, for that matter, you cannot make other people care that your favourite dancer has ineffable movement quality. These things must speak for themselves.

At this point many people may argue against my bothering to write about something that seems second rate. Here they are mistaken. The satirical humour of **The Concert** requires an acquaintance with the world of ballet while **Jeux de Cartes** appeals on an instinctive level, but I laughed just as much at **The Concert**.

What art could be less pure than a drama about events which have occurred in our lives? Mere editing of reproduced happenings, a far cry from art for art's sake. Yet drama is one of our most powerful art forms. The story is in the telling, and this involves the mundane as well as the extraordinary because the latter would be nothing without the former. Doubtless many choreographers would protest that it is not their business to tell stories, but we are fortunate that alongside their abstract ballets we have also a few great dramatic ones.

For the most part, then, my subject here is the aspect of some of the most beautiful and touching of all ballets which relates directly to our everyday lives. It is the humbler aspect of the dance, its human touch.

GISELLE

Every aspiring ballerina wants to dance it, every woman who was once an innocent girl is moved by its performances, and it has inspired an enormous amount of literature and analysis. The oldest ballet to have been continuously performed invokes real passion in large numbers of people. It has a universal appeal despite the fact that it belongs irreparably to a bygone era. To the uninitiated this must all seem utterly insane. What is the secret of this artificial and unrealistic old warhorse, which makes it live for people here and now?

Obviously it is the character of Giselle herself that bridges the gap between the ages. Why does she appeal more than, say, Juliet?

I believe that I can answer for the women, at least: every one of us has been Giselle. She is a fundamental part of each of us. Anyone who has been an unhappy child without knowing why, and anyone who in her first romantic encounter has learned why, has been Giselle. Even anyone who has never had a romantic encounter knows what betrayal would mean to her, and anyone else has experienced it already to some degree, because other people will not always conform to our fantasies. Juliet's experience, on the other hand, is quite uncommon. Oddly, it is Juliet who impresses us as being made of flesh and blood, for her grief is not the gossamer of a child's hurt feelings while Giselle's vulnerability is a thing of unbearable fragility. But though Giselle is a ghost, we who have survived her experience find that ghost within ourselves.

After being spoilt for such a little, little time, why does Giselle have to bear her dreadful penance, as if she has no right to her bit of happiness? Is it so much to ask that you may be everything to another person, when he is everything to you? After her betrayal, Giselle is expected to return to her childhood, having tasted the joys of womanhood, and childhood is not enough. She is no longer thought beautiful. She is alone again. If she cries, his arms will not encircle her. He will not care, and he will not come. Before, he would have appeared concerned over the tiniest hurt. Now, to everyone but her mother she is just another person. Before, she basked in her sudden fame. For a brief moment she lived as previously she had only heard of others living. The sun shone on her world and made it beautiful. Now all that is gone. She is supposed to face her old life again, in the same world, without that sun.

Throughout this ballet, we seem to be experiencing two dramas, Giselle's and our own. The music acts as a link between them, reaching into the audience as the action cannot. The visual message is distant. Our past lives are being re-enacted within the picturesque frame of the proscenium, before our very eyes —not as events happened physically, but as they were experienced by us at the time. The pastoral setting of the first act is a pictorial representation of the subjective world of a young girl in love, the world as seen through Giselle's eyes. Herein lies the secret of the ballet's enduring success: it is psychologically sound. All settings and circumstances are perfectly appropriate. Giselle as an individual does not exist. She is a personification of innocence. In the diegesis of the ballet she is parallel to each of us in a world long past. And she dies, as each of us died.

In her resurrection as a wili Giselle is forever changed. Her world is beautiful because her pain is beautiful. The wind whispering among rustling leaves and moonlight filtering through dark branches are no pathetic fallacy; we are reliving the experience of being Giselle. We see everything through her eyes. We are looking at the landscape of a mind.

Every woman who views the events taking place in the sunny open space by Giselle's cottage is seeing them for the second time. In order to inspire emotion an artist must reproduce its circumstances. If an audience member has previously felt such an emotion this will produce the desired result, and if she has not then the effort has proven futile. The effort is fruitful in Giselle because we were all born innocent, and because innocents expect other people to fulfill all their dreams —in fact, to have no minds of their own. Innocents are doomed to the disillusionment which is necessary for their maturation and for the development of a true ability to love others as they really are. Only some of us can relate to Juliet's mortal agony as she drags her dying body across the floor of her tomb. After all, many people have not yet experienced the death of a loved one. But every adult, woman or man, has known the death of a dream.

Jules Perrot, in creating the title role, seems to have relished vicarious suffering. This begins as soon as we discover Albrecht's true identity, and it builds each time Giselle is reassured by him in the first act. If she were perfectly trusting, his crime would not be so terrible. Imagine her feelings when Hilarion discloses Albrecht's duplicity. She has feared a less catastrophic event but has never truly believed it would occur. At first she is confused, only dimly aware that something is terribly wrong, and that her man is in the middle of it. Her pleasure at his central position is being displaced every second by a growing dread. Perhaps she has on other occasions wished to be the central character in a dramatic situation, but now she fervently wishes that this could all prove to be a farce. Hilarion places the aristocrat's horn to his lips. Giselle's body seems to belong to another person. This must be a dream. Bathilde's party begins to arrive, and the end of Giselle's happiness. Every moment seems to last an eternity as we see innocence destroyed before our eyes.

But now imagine Albrecht's feelings throughout the first act. He is not an indecisive person. However, he has made an irresponsible mistake in allowing Giselle to convince herself that he wants to marry her. He wishes that he had never put both of them in this position, and he will never forget the lesson he has learned from this vulnerable creature whom he desperately wishes to protect. Her pain upon discovering that he has another life is exasercbated by the fact that in her mind his only identity has been as her lover. She has never pictured him with another woman. She has never thought of him as a person in his own right, and that is not his fault.

His error lies in the fact that he has let the matter ride. He knows Giselle cannot understand that his feelings for her are separate from his relationship with Bathilde. When he was initially drawn to this young girl, he did not realize what her hopes were. He thought that his attentiveness was kind and indulgent. By the time he knew better, it was too late for him to tell the truth without causing a total collapse. True, the longer he waits the worse the outcome, but he may suspect that it will be fatal anyway. Why not allow the poor girl a few more moments of bliss?

He may have resolved to bare all on numerous occasions, knowing that carrying on the charade would only cause her to fall harder in the end. But how could he, seeing that bright little person, flushed with joy, gazing up at him with utter devotion? For the very reason that he did care for her, he could not cause that small round face to crumple. The situation has been getting worse and worse. The longer this goes on, the more terrible his crime becomes. With each reassurance, a deeper level of pain is ascribed to the inevitable fall.

Albrecht has never considered marrying Giselle and flying in the face of the obligations imposed upon him from childhood. He will not reach her level of passion and commitment until he has seen her die, too late to make amends. He has put himself in a double bind. His only sin is procrastination. But he refuses to accept his responsibility to deal with reality because he is a merciful person. If it were up to him, Giselle would never find out the truth. He refuses to accept the fact that somehow or other she is bound to discover who he really is, because other people will not be so kind. He pretends that things can go on forever as they are. He wants Giselle to have her happiness as long as she can. It is to his credit that at least he does not run when Hilarion blows the horn, because he must want to very, very much. Yes, Perrot definitely had a sadistic streak.

It is interesting to note that Giselle makes a man of Albrecht. However she is not transformed into a woman, becoming only a shadow of her former self. We may have grown up after our innocence was shattered, but Giselle exists only as a personification of this innocence itself. Albrecht, on the other hand, begins the ballet as a compromising person and ends it as an uncompromising one. Ironically, only Giselle's death can prompt him into this character development, thus trapping him forever into the marriage of convenience he has renounced too late. And as a newly responsible person, he is obliged to go through with it. The ballet can be seen entirely as the story of Albrecht's maturation and redemption. At the beginning of the ballet he was not willing to go the full nine yards in order to defy convention, and his is a story of personal growth. Since he is as central to the plot as Giselle herself, many critics have observed that the work could as easily have been entitled **Albrecht**. And it is not inappropriate that this ballet has been called the **Hamlet** of the dance, for though the Danish prince is steadfast against corruption, both characters waver when having to choose between unacceptable evils.

Throughout the action, Bathilde acts as an aristocrat should. She is distinctly a stranger to us, because we see her through Giselle's eyes. Her admirable maturity only belittles the poor girl more, but Bathilde is totally blameless. She even goes so far as to fetch Albrecht from the forest at the end of the ballet. Her appearance at the end of Act II is significant. Albrecht has learned to deal with reality, and he belongs with his future wife. Otherwise, ironically, his redemption can mean nothing. Besides, Giselle's sacrifice in the second act involves handing him over to Bathilde, knowing that she will thus ensure for herself a special place in his heart as a perfect memory, something his wife can never be. Bathilde is a powerful figure in Act I, for Giselle is doubly betrayed when she discovers that her rival is not only Albrecht's true betrothed, but also an aristocrat like himself. She has fondly imagined that he was proud of his association with her, while in fact he was one of Bathilde's class, viewing her as a person of low rank. There never was any serious consideration that she might be worthy of him. Giselle is triply betrayed when she recalls entertaining Bathilde with the news of her own engagement –her false engagement to the man whom, in fact, Bathilde is going to marry. And Bathilde's kindness and graciousness only rub salt in the wound.

How Giselle blushed, how her eyes sparkled, how she bowed her head shyly to hide the fact that she was enormously pleased, thinking all the while that her man must be far better in every way than Bathilde's, despite the latter's position. She felt a sisterhood with this exalted personage, now revealed to be her victorious rival. How vain she must appear, presuming herself the equal of a noblewoman. How cruel it is that she must be humiliated in front of a rival who is hopelessly beyond her reach. And what a little fool she has made of herself in front of this very woman. She even regretted her lover's absence during Bathilde's visit, when of course he was making himself scarce on purpose. Every honour bestowed upon her in her happiness acquired meaning only because of Albrecht, because she was his beloved, because it was important to him. The praise of her dancing and the gift of pearls seem patronizing now, and her crowning as queen of the grape harvest (the pinnacle of her joy immediately before the fall) is remembered now as a scene from which Albrecht was conspicuously absent.

Hilarion holds a position of importance in his community, and is insulted by Giselle's lack of interest in him. He sincerely believes that he is good for her, and convinces himself that exposing Albrecht is the right thing to do. Unlike his more sensitive rival, he has no idea of the effect this will produce. He is free to despise Albrecht as his jealousy dictates, arguing that he does so for Giselle's sake. We can tell that it is Giselle's open rejection which really motivates his actions. Giselle never thinks once about the pain she is causing Hilarion. If I were to credit him with knowing what harm he was doing, I would suspect that he wanted revenge on Giselle. As it is, he is the direct instrument of her collapse. Because we see through the girl's eyes, Hilarion's drama is downplayed. We do not care how he feels during Act I, and his death in Act II is passed over quickly without any of the sympathy involved in Albrecht's ordeal. Remember that we are looking into Giselle's mind. Hilarion is murdered because to that mind he is dispensable.

Nobody was ever in love with Hilarion. Albrecht is a different matter. It is hard to kill someone with whom you are romantically involved, even if he has betrayed you. Since it is impossible to recall the past, only one alternative is left. Giselle's nobility in the second act takes an interesting form. It just happens to place her in a position of power over Albrecht's very life. Perrot must have intended the role reversal involved in her gently bending to lift Albrecht's exhausted body from the ground. She does not appear vindictive. Her self image has taken enough beating already without turning to ugliness.

But I slip into pragmatism. It is important to resist this error in analyzing the ballet. Giselle is not a character who masquerades as a forgiving spirit; nor is she the puppeteer who places a symbol of herself on the stage acting out her wishes. We are merely being presented with a story which corresponds to what happens in an innocent young girl's mind when she is betrayed in love, and the last thing I wish to do is deny the beauty of this second act. It is noble, and it is moving. Yet its images are appropriate to the mental wanderings of a young girl with a broken heart, and this is not by accident.

We are presented with two aspects of Giselle that shimmer in front of us, one commanding our attention, the other fleetingly intruding —the gentle, pious figure in the white dress that we see before our eyes, and the underlying psychological interpretation. We must consciously choose the former, and conclude that Giselle is as she appears —a personification of broken innocence, an image. We must remember that she was always Perrot's creation, and is not representative of a person you could actually meet. Giselle is not vindictive because this would destroy her beauty. Nevertheless, everything works out according to what would be her fantasy if she were a real person. Hilarion is killed. Albrecht is punished, and she has become to him something that Bathilde can never be, without ever having to test whether it is of greater value to him. In a poignant irony, Giselle must wistfully fade away into her grave at the appearance of the same thin ray of sunlight which saves Albrecht. In a way, he is being rejected in his turn, although this is thin consolation for a broken heart.

What is her real consolation? What cushions the blow a little to make a death-in-life bearable when you have lost a romance? Let us think a little about what this romance has meant to Giselle. For the first time she has been seen as beautiful and desirable —by someone she wants, that is, since Hilarion doesn't count. This view of herself, which she imagines Albrecht to cherish, she supposes to have been adopted by other villagers. The assumption of everyone else's interest is typical of someone in Giselle's mental state. In fact, it is Giselle who has seen herself as beautiful and desirable. It is her self image which was affected by Albrecht's attentions, and it is her self image which has been shattered. The only solace can be the creation of an alternative view of herself as equally beautiful. What can be beautiful about a little fool of a peasant girl who has been rejected as unworthy? Her spirit of forgiveness. Giselle's only bearable alternative is sainthood. So profound was Perrot's understanding of feminine psychology in recognizing this fact that I strongly suspect some uncredited contribution from Carlotta Grisi, the first ballerina to dance Giselle.

Poor Myrthe did not make the same choice. Her dance at the beginning of Act II, far from being a stern distraction, is actually a gentle comment on the unspeakable sadness of someone who has refused to learn from her experiences. There is an immovable quietude at her heart, but it is the quiet of an empty place. She is a nun without vocation, living a death-in-life of endless denial. Myrthe is a foil for Giselle, whose decision to become a beautiful person counter-acts her being made to feel less than beautiful beside another woman. Myrthe and her wilis are all less beautiful than Giselle. The choice Giselle makes is a noble one, and I say this without cynicism. There is no point in criticizing her, as she does not exist outside her ballet, except as a part of ourselves who lives forever in our hearts. We must take her religious grace at face value over and above its psychological interpretation. Of the two aspects presented to us we must choose the figure of forgiveness and undying devotion.

If the dancer portraying Giselle recalls her own personal experience, every nuance becomes a retracing of steps already taken. Theoretically, any dancer would be able to move an audience to tears with the appropriate gestures, but would have to be carefully coached. A ballerina who has never felt Giselle's emotions will probably not be involved enough in her story to make the appropriate gestures, which require that she discard the mask of invulnerability each of us wears. She will simply not be motivated sufficiently to take such a step. But dancers know that in their profession people seldom look remotely close to the way they feel, and when Giselle expresses emotion she must do so with her head at a certain angle and her feet carefully positioned. Her physiognomy must be a faithful embodiment of her psychology and both are understood together or not at all.

One ballerina might capture Giselle's sweetness and simplicity. Another might allow us to see that she is a self centred child who considers others only insofar as they relate to herself. Giselle is vulnerable because she cares about herself quite obsessively. Everyone around her is defined in accordance with a role played in her life. How shocking it must be when the roles are shuffled, when Albrecht ceases to be her lover, when Bathilde ceases to be her sisterly benefactor, and when Hilarion ceases to be merely Albrecht's foil, a role which he has so bitterly resented. Giselle sees herself in the same manner, as she is reflected in others' eyes. She has defined herself in terms of a role, and the shuffle creates an identity crisis.

Giselle resembles a porcelain figurine more than a

real peasant girl. She is light in frame, though the conventions of the Romantic era require that she be softly padded, without angularity. She has little soft hands with short fingers, baby hands. And while babies have beautifully positioned fingers, nevertheless a baby's hands are not deft or capable. Each finger seems to move on its own, dainty but not adept. Her feet are likewise small, and seem to move with a life of their own under her full skirt. Unconsciously she places them in closed, turned out positions, though it is acceptable to depart from this convention, even stepping heel first upon occasion, to demonstrate her gaucherie.

Tradition dictates that Giselle should have a slender waist, but I think a childish figure would be quite appropriate for her. Tradition dictates also that she must have sloping shoulders, yet thin, straight little shoulders would be very appealing also. When she descends into her grave at the end of the second act she raises them in a childlike gesture as she holds her arms, full of lilies, above her head. In repose she stands with her back arched uncomfortably at the waist like a small child, her shoulders back and her neck forward. Her head is set on a disproportionately thin neck, for all the world like a lollipop. Her elbows tend to be held lower than her wrists to avoid an appearance of strength in the upper back. If a dancer does not meet the physical requirements of the role she can nevertheless remain so true to Giselle's character in her movements that her physique only adds a new dimension to her interpretation.

For it is true that any girl can be Giselle. Any unconventional appearance, such as approaching middle age, can add pathos to the story. A dancer who is not endowed with childish features suggesting innocence need not despair of ever portraying Giselle. She can tilt and bob her head shyly in the first act, and she can arch her neck to gaze adoringly at Albrecht. She can also set her face into the unguarded expression of a baby, and may even find that large or sharp features inspire sympathy in her audience.

The ideal face for Giselle would, of course, be the face of a baby —a round face, with a small nose and chin. Hers is not a model's pout, with the muscles around the mouth relaxed and the membrane itself curling outward. The muscles around the mouth are pushing out, but the lips themselves remain thin. The mouth opens as a result, pursing at both corners and creating dimples. Rounded cheeks with soft little deposits of excess fat on the inner sides, near the nose, convey a childlike appearance. Such deposits create faint shadows in a young girl between the sides of the nose and the corners of the mouth, though they harden into lines with age. In preparing for Act I, rouge applied to the inner cheeks rather than to the cheekbones will emphasize this facial shape. The resulting impression is one of unguarded innocence, without any intensity. Place one hand on each cheek before a mirror and press inward, and you will see the same effect.

Yet some of the greatest exponents of this role were not endowed with soft, childlike features and nevertheless excelled at portraying innocence. Perhaps their secret was an understanding that Giselle is not embarrassed at displaying her emotions. She does not employ the techniques of the world-wise in disguising her enthusiasms and disappointments. Her face is not a mask. Picasso painted such a face in a canvas entitled **First Step**, depicting a baby (centrally positioned, as babies always are) with a concerned mother's face on the periphery. The baby has an eager expression, one which knows nothing of the sins in this world. Who would be so cruel as to introduce evil into the baby's life, and cause that little face to crumple? Any face can take on this vulnerability, as long as its owner is brave enough to allow it.

Have you ever seen anyone who never thought she would be admired? By someone she wants, that is. Giselle is such a character. Her delighted response upon encountering courtship (from someone she wants) is mixed with timidity, because she finds the whole thing hard to believe. Why should she allow her expectations to be raised if they are only to be brought down again? Clearly, Giselle is not an arrogant girl, despite her treatment of Hilarion. In fact, she is very flattered by Albrecht's attentions. Her lip quivers. She adjusts her hair self consciously, suddenly finding reason to be aware of an appearance which she had never deemed worthy of note. She employs few head movements and is slow to change focus. She can scarcely take her eyes off Albrecht in either act. Except during the 'mad' scene, her gaze is fixed upon him every moment that he is present. During the first act she is uneasy whenever he is absent, except for just one moment of unexpected glory when she is crowned queen of the harvest, and it seems that she is punished for this brief lapse of attention. In the second act, she is immovably self contained whether he is present or not, having found peace, accepting her fate with dignity and forgiveness —no longer clinging and dependent. Giselle's torso seldom leans toward Albrecht in either act, even though she constantly looks in his direction. Such extreme behaviour would be too rude a departure from Romantic conventions.

The 'mad' scene has its own special body language. It is very difficult to achieve the effect of a tremor running through one's entire frame, but this is required, particularly toward the very end of the scene, when Giselle turns from her mother's arms to see a distraught Albrecht. A hesitation before the tremor reaches a peak will heighten its impact, indicating Giselle's new uncertainty over her reception and her inability to trust Albrecht. A sensitive partner will extend his arms again in a welcoming gesture. This he will do rather pathetically, knowing that the condition of his welcome is its temporary nature, and fully aware that he is not offering very much.

No such nuance is necessary upon Giselle's first discovery of her betrayal. She just stands helplessly with arms at her sides and a fixed expression on her face, which seems to be collapsing around a central point, her brows sloping downward from the middle and her mouth drawn upward. When she separates Albrecht and Bathilde, she cannot stop shaking her head in disbelief. Preliminary study of the appropriate movement patterns is important in order that they may be adopted by habit, leaving the performers free to become emotionally involved without the distraction of constantly thinking about correct positioning.

This leads me to the rather tiresome issue of taste. Dancers are often cautioned to 'tone down' their performances in **Giselle**. It is never appropriate that Giselle be inhibited. Of course she does not tear out her hair and beat her breast. She is a fragile thing, a creature of gentleness and sensitivity, and violence is so alien to her that the most forceful thing she does is collapse. She cannot break the laws of her ballet. The absurdity of anachronism would shatter the audience's suspension of disbelief. But this ballet is more than a period piece, and it does not deserve to have its heart ripped out.

There is one way to deal with this so-called problem, and this is recognizing that Giselle is a personification of innocence, with a limited vocabulary of gestures. Expressing oneself within her framework must become second nature. We are all creatures of habit who find it easy to slip into conventions –just think how easy it is to face one direction on the traditional stage. The dancer must then throw caution to the wind and perform the role with abandon, and she cannot go wrong. A mistake is impossible if she is Giselle somewhere inside, and has brought her to the fore. As long as she is locked into the conventions of a ballet stage in the 1840s, she can let loose within their confines, without the slightest inclination to do anything inappropriate. If she understands Giselle's despair she will carry the audience with her, but if she uses the people watching her as a mirror, her image shall do no more than bounce off them ineffectively. She must forget that she is in a theatre trying to make an impression, and must be unafraid of appearing a fool.

How can she project without overly exaggerating? Consider the colours of aquamarine and ultramarine. The same subtlety is required in mixing green and blue to produce either, because the ratio is the same in both, yet ultramarine is a considerably darker shade. Ultramarine is not less refined; it simply has more colour. In **Giselle** subtlety, precision and careful timing are indispensable, but magnification of each movement is required. This exaggerated acting style was typical of nineteenth century theatre and gradually fell out of vogue during the twentieth, due to the advent of film. It is not only totally appropriate in **Giselle**; it is absolutely authentic. This ballet is a melodrama —one of picturesque delicacy, but definitely a melodrama. Although we are far removed from the action, it is not frivolous entertainment, and the performers' movements are not much larger than those of people experiencing deep emotion.

We are always being told that the title role is difficult to dance because of the difference between the two acts. Yet Giselle is not a stranger in Act II. Before she throws off her veil there is a moment of trepidation during which I always wonder what she is going to look like, this shadow of the young girl who was so very, very alive. Have you ever been afraid to meet someone who has been through a cataclysmic tragedy? There is a horror, a desire to avoid the confrontation. Who knows what changes may have taken place? But the shadow, when unveiled, has acquired a new beauty. The dark enormities of her eyes are set in an ashen face, but she is still the same spirit who existed, gay and blithe, within her little body.

The first act is full of fine touches which can easily be ruined. Take for example the first mime scene between Giselle and Albrecht. Giselle bumps into him, turns and blushes, rather flustered as she hurriedly smoothes her skirt, completely out of breath. She has been caught off guard, but she is dimpling and is obviously thrilled to the toes. This coy little creature is probably difficult to court, very shy and also intent upon testing her lover, but she is entirely his without reservation, and is utterly transparent about the fact. Giselle can fool nobody. The audience already guesses how terrible a betrayal would be, and we don't really need to overplay the game that she plays with daisy petals. The foreshadowing is there already –Giselle is able to guess that there is an even number of petals on her daisy without poring over it– and when Albrecht plucks an odd number from his to reassure her, we are still left with uncertainty. Giselle cannot really believe that her lover is unfaithful. The prospect is too horrendous to be seriously considered. Consequently, her doubt must be given a very light touch.

She is still a bit afraid of this alien being which confronts her, and hence Albrecht's little problem getting her to sit close to him on the bench. She is breathless still, her head turned slightly away, a little smile on her face and a sparkle in her eye which she thinks he does not see. She is afraid at her own daring. All the wonderful things she has heard of are now happening to her. The little differences between lovers might happen too. So, leaving a small space between them, she picks a daisy and plucks off a petal, trying out her charms by looking at him from the corner of her eye. She has never employed her wiles before and is delighted to find them successful. She plucks a 'no', another 'yes', and stops. What if he doesn't really love her? She has heard of such things. She stands, her body rigid, not daring to look at him. But he reassures her, and one glance at his gently teasing expression is enough. Like a baby animal she is volatile, one second afraid and the next wildly happy. Suddenly elated, she skips around the stage grasping his hand with one baby fist, making him dance with her.

The waltz should be performed in the same spirit. Its music captures the essence of Giselle's sunny euphoria. Her feet seem to carry her like two birds in flight, separate from the rest of her body, moving so fast they are barely visible. (The costumes and movement style for ballerinas of the Romantic era make this effect possible.) As she and Albrecht break away from the dance, he becomes distracted and enters a conversation with someone else. Giselle (always by his side) takes his hand as before, looking happily at the dancing figures, letting everyone see that she is with him. Happy, she looks up at Albrecht and sees that he is preoccupied.

This is all right for a couple of seconds. She looks at his companion, then back at him, and sees that he is capable of becoming engrossed in someone else. She, on the other hand, thinks of him every moment. When he is present, she is always aware of where he is and what he is doing. She slips silently away, tense and frightened, her body unmoving from the waist up. Her eyes are large, her neck a little too far forward, and her weak heart is palpitating dangerously. A couple of onlookers see her and one glances at Albrecht, but neither does anything. He fails to notice until a second later, when he turns to look for her and tenderly puts his arm around her shoulders. Instantly delighted, she pulls him into the dance's finale which begins with all the young people side by side in a line, Giselle at one end and Albrecht at the other, all the time Giselle laughing across everyone's heads at the man she loves and having a little difficulty keeping up. Her eyes do not depart from him for an instant.

After the finale, eager to show off her accomplishments, she insists on continuing. He lets her go, and she runs around into the solo leading to their duet. During this duet, as the two dance the same steps hand in hand, Giselle's ballon comes from strength in her feet, not from her demi plie. She is not elastic. Her movements are not smooth. She flits over the surface of the stage floor. It may even be admissible to add a few extra steps, since Giselle is smaller than Albrecht and is thoroughly excited –instead of a hop, balloné step and grand jeté, a hop, balloné, three fast steps and grand jeté. As she dances, Giselle's eyes do not leave Albrecht, causing her to appear ecstatic when inclined toward him and coquettish when inclined away.

When Giselle is crowned queen of the grape harvest, her joy is a culmination of many things, heaped upon her happiness in love. She is to find that without that foundation those things mean nothing to her. It is for us to note the conspicuous absence of Albrecht. I think it would be inappropriate for anything but delight to shine upon Giselle's face at this time. She is not a miserable creature, after all.

Now that we come to the 'mad' scene, I think that a bar by bar analysis is appropriate:

14 bars –Hilarion arrives from upstage left behind the hut where Albrecht has hidden his belongings. He stubbornly gesticulates, as a decent man who has been offended by the sins of another, while Albrecht ineffectively tries to quiet him, not suspecting how much his enemy really knows. Hilarion mimes his accusation and bolts inside the hut. Albrecht grabs him, but Hilarion has brought out the sword, cloak and horn. Giselle is bewildered and worried but still trusting and protective of her admirer. Even now, not understanding the situation, she may feel some enjoyment in the fact that her lover is the centre of everyone's attention.

1 bar —Hilarion blows the horn and Albrecht, seeing that his fate is sealed, brings his arms down.

9 bars —The Duke, Bathilde and their entourage enter from upstage right. Albrecht makes furtive gestures to Bathilde and the Duke indicating that he wants them to deny that they know him, but both of them are watching Hilarion questioningly. Hilarion gestures toward Albrecht, who cannot hide. Bathilde steps toward him extending her hand, head inclined, in recognition and with some surprise.

6 bars —Giselle runs between them, erratically shaking her head. She stands half toward Albrecht, half toward the audience —every muscle tense, every nerve alert. She stares imploringly at Albrecht, but he appears frozen. She shifts her weight from one foot to the other, still shaking her head, her face contorting more and more until it collapses entirely as she utters a silent cry and blindly runs forward toward stage right. She has nowhere to go, but she cannot stay where she is. She trips over her own feet, totters and falls on her face in a bundle.

3 bars —People edge nervously toward each other when Giselle fails to pick herself up. The fall has been the last straw for her. Slowly, slowly she lifts her head, and her face looks frozen, not like Giselle's face at all. Her body convulses, terrifying the onlookers. They move into a semicircle around her, mute and humble, as though a ritual were taking place. Giselle stands unsteadily, wavering slightly, racked by periodic tremors, her face drawn. Her legs are slightly apart, her arms rather gauchely bent at her sides, unmoving. From now on they will continue to be bent in this helpless manner.

12 bars –Still shaken, Giselle absent mindedly mimes holding a daisy in her left hand and plucking its petals with her right. She moves very slowly, nodding her head wonderingly after one imaginary petal is removed, shaking it likewise after the next. Her eyes stare at nothing, her head is inclined slightly. Nobody else moves but Albrecht who, alone understanding the significance of her gestures, drops his head in shame. Giselle plucks no more than four petals, ending with a 'no', and as she suddenly realizes that the 'no' is real, her face crumples. Both hands fly to cover it.

6 bars –Through her fingers Giselle sees Albrecht's sword lying nearby, and in a stupor she picks it up. She is too stunned to be aware of the fact that she is holding it by the blade. Bent slightly forward, feet in an imperfect third position, grasping the blade with both fists, she stares into nothing, desperate yet unmoving, as a wild plan takes place in her numbed brain. Her face is no longer impassive. A fierce excitement and determination mingled with fear are breaking through the mask. This effect is accomplished by opening the eyes very wide without moving the lower half of the face. Extending the transformation to the jawline would constitute a departure from the Romantic conventions which are inseparable from Giselle's character; she retains to the end her sensitive mouth.

Her mixed feelings are clearly mounting within her small frame, the spirit overcoming her frail body. This effect is accomplished by hyperventilating, raising the shoulders and arms slightly with each breath. Her eyes are bright with terror, her gaze fixed upward. Dreading what she is about to do, yet more afraid of having the weapon taken away, she runs in a circle dragging the hilt of the sword along the stage floor. She must appear driven to do this as a leaf is borne by the wind, with no apparent muscular force.

Without warning, she tries to drive the point into her chest, using both hands, but the sword is taken from her. This is yet another violation to her feelings, and the expression of shock and hurt returns. A shudder pervades her frame. Suddenly with her lost, drawn face and half bent body, clutching the sword blade to her chest, she seems a dejected little figure. Aimlessly her feet carry her sideways, a trifle off balance. She regains her equilibrium and stares, puzzled and stunned. Some readers might think that all these developments cannot fit into a mere six bars. The truth is that they feel like the longest six bars in the ballet.

17 bars –Giselle's full awareness of the situation returns now that her resolve has subsided with the loss of the sword. She returns to her mourning, face stricken, eyes large and shining. Falteringly she repeats the steps that she and Albrecht danced so happily before, and she imagines that he is joining her. She repeats the balloné sequence from their duet for five bars, with stricken face and tragic eyes as she mimics its alternating coquettish and ecstatic expressions. Her smile of remembrance is a terrible thing to see. But the smile is becoming genuine by the fifth repetition of the sequence as Giselle forgets her present situation and becomes lost in her memory.

4 bars –She does not complete the expected number of repetitions. Instead, she stops at the end of the fifth, suddenly brought back to reality with her defenses down. She has suddenly remembered that things are not as they were, that everything is dif-

ferent, that she is not to Albrecht what she thought she was —that he is engaged to Bathilde, that it is all gone, no more. And she strokes the air as though gently, gently touching Albrecht's cheek. She does this hesitantly, with infinite tenderness, as though afraid to sully his perfection with an insensitive gesture. Then her other hand, like a lover's, guides the first to her own cheek. Inclining her head toward it with a slight nuzzling movement, eyes closed in a sort of ecstasy, she imagines she is holding Albrecht's hand to her face, as though it were the most precious object in the world. Yet she is not lost in a memory this time, and there is no smile on her face. She is not remembering, but rather is expressing her wish that she may know such tenderness. In this most poignant moment, the very air seems to quiver.

6 bars —Suddenly Giselle loses all control. This grief is too much for her. Being Albrecht's beloved meant everything to her, and now there is nothing left. Stumbling a little, she steps toward the people whom she has just noticed around her, groping for any support, though obviously her hands will not resemble grasping claws. Her fingers are outstretched and separate, and her feet are slightly turned out — after years of rigorous training this will be second nature to any ballerina and will in no way detract from her involvement in the moment.

Seeing Albrecht first she appeals to him, then remembering that he does not love her she turns away. Hilarion is seen next and she starts to move toward him, but she remembers that he was the one who cruelly disclosed the terrible truth. She searches the throng with her eyes, pleading that she might find someone to whom she is as important as she was to Albrecht. She makes more than a half circle around, pleading for a pair of outstretched arms to answer hers, and in the far corner they wait for her, the arms that held her as a child. Although her mother's love does not hold the promise of a glorious future, it is the only love by which she is central in someone's life. And it is a love which will not let her down. In fact, her mother is the one person who warned Giselle and tried to protect her from this moment. Giselle sees those arms, and she speeds toward them as naturally as any injured animal comes home. She seems to collapse across the stage instead of downward, and she lands in her mother's embrace as if a superhuman force has transported her where she needs to be.

Albrecht wishes to make amends, with genuine remorse. He is not seeking forgiveness. He truly wants to assure Giselle that he is sorry for what he has done, and with this in mind he has stepped toward her. At his approach, she suddenly seems to implode. Her hands jerk spasmodically over her face as she collapses. This time as she falls the movement is entirely vertical, which is not hard to achieve as Albrecht is trying to hold her up.

12 bars –The orchestra breaks into the dramatic theme to which Hilarion first disclosed Albrecht's secret, producing an effect of coming full circle. This is 'showdown' music. I wish that Perrault had given it to Giselle, so that before she fell she could slowly, slowly turn to Albrecht. Wanting him to care about what has happened, but afraid of what she will see in his face, she would be drawn to look in hope of seeing a glimmer of affection. She would dart one glance of undying devotion, see the remorse on his face, and (for all the world like a wife) in genuine compassion she would begin to stretch her arms

toward him. In her last moments of life, she would have changed. She would actually be sorry for him. Desperately he would open his arms, wildly grateful for a chance to console her, and we would see the beginning of their transformed relationship in the second act. But before her arms were fully stretched, Giselle would remember that she was the little peasant girl who had been jilted, and doubted the welcome she will receive. This could be a moment of great pathos. He would still pleading, with arms outstretched, and she would rush into them. Each would seek the other's support, and they would literally hold each other up, offering each other strength.

Giselle would be the stronger, cradling her desolate lover's head in her arms. But as the music reaches a new peak like a cry of pain, her head would sink onto his, seemingly from the intensity of her love. Her head would be inclined toward the audience, but the face would not be visible. Her legs would bend at the knees, with pointed feet, and her hands would slip down to Albrecht's waist, loosening their hold. Even though she would be the one collapsing, he would be humbled before her. Upon the reiteration of the cry, her head would fall back and we would see that we were mistaken about the reason for her collapse, that in fact she had died of a heart attack. Words cannot convey the impact of these two musical peals, and it would be most effective to have one with Giselle slumped over her lover, and the other as her head falls back. All her weight would be on Albrecht's arms and her head would be unsupported, allowing the shoulders to be raised. Her body would form a crescent shape, back arched, feet still pointed behind her. Her arms would still be bent in front of her, hands open as if wanting to embrace her lover even in death, as with great tenderness he lowered her body.

Unfortunately for my vision, the original choreography for this music is given to Albrecht. Giselle's mother mourns over her daughter, forcing Albrecht to step back in shame, and he realizes in desperation that he is powerless to reverse the harm that has been done. He briefly blames Hilarion and is hurried away from this place in which he is unwelcome. Freed from their shock, the village folk are overcome by grief.

The music for **Giselle** is of immense importance. Entirely bound by convention, it remains pretty and predictable throughout, like a sort of homily. Romantic ballet music slavishly follows every mood in the main line of action. The result is a certain triviality. Let us take the overture, for example. The beginning is very excited indeed, without warning, indicating that the events about to unfold will be melodramatic. Then it settles down to a quaintly rustic theme, preparing us for the first act. Overtures of the period often take this form, opening with a general commentary on what we are about to witness, then setting the mood (always contrastingly quiet) for the opening scene. In this case the form is so obvious as to be almost silly, but it performs its function to perfection. Then there is Albrecht's first entrance — strings and brass, with considerable energy. This must be our hero. After assuming his disguise, he turns toward Giselle's cottage. We hear strings. The music softens as he places a hand over his heart, and it supplies us with taps on the door most obligingly. There is a musical uproar when Hilarion first tries to separate the lovers, and still more the second time, when he is successful. The peasants' entrance is unmistakable, with strong emphasis on tuba and cellos; no more so than the entrance of the aristocrats, with its horns and violins.

The music acts as a sort of mirror and magnifying glass combined, parallel to the action on stage, and also amplifying it. If we were to miss anything on stage (which would be highly unlikely) the music would inform us as a commentator. When the tiny figures beyond the proscenium appear agitated the music torrents in our ears. It brings the action nearer, reminds us that we are not just spectators. As those pretty figures dance on a distant stage, another drama is enacted within each of us, expressed by sounds which the tiny characters do not hear. Sometimes the music seems to lose control of itself, seems to forget its place in the world of picturesque entertainment, trying to be more dramatic than it can adequately manage. **Giselle** would be ridiculous if it were not sublime.

In 1841 ballet was a light affair. The story of **Giselle** might have been frivolous, if not taken seriously by Perrot. His contribution raised the ballet to a new level. Consider the fact that the famous pas de deux at the end of Act II is not endowed with music one can describe as deeply moving by itself. Yet our memory of the carefree variations from Act I clings to the figures of Giselle and Albrecht and transforms this moment into one of crystalline beauty. The rigid choreographic conventions intensify the impact rather than detracting from it, just as the smaller the area on which a given weight is laid, the greater becomes the pressure. And last but not least, the prettiness of sets and costumes serves a dramatic purpose as the landscape of Giselle's mind.

Giselle is a ballet that did forget its place, and became far greater than the sum of its parts. The music is tuneful, the story has great possibilities, the choreography belongs to its time, and the sets are idyllic. But together, together they can break your heart.

ROMEO AND JULIET

Romeo and Juliet is a less perfect but more ambitious work than **Giselle**. This is a searing, passionate, powerful, violent, BIG story. But it has its problems.

Even for twentieth century choreographers Prokofiev's music was challenging. Once dubbed "impossible to dance to", it has received many choreographic treatments over the years, all of them flawed. Lavrovsky's original version was created before Russia became acquainted with modern dance forms, but its sweeping style more than compensates. Macmillan and Cranko, who borrowed heavily from the original, incorporated the modern return to basics into their choreography, aware of the contrasting forces involved in all movement. Consequently, in their work these forces become deliberately and obviously apparent.

The depth and power of the choreography is well suited to a ballet with wilful and daring protagonists. The inevitability of their fate does not alter the fact that they are its most active instruments, that they work very hard within its framework, lacking the fatal flaw which seals the fate of Othello and Hamlet. The lovers' decisions require great courage, and appear to be predestined only in the sense that they are true to their deepest convictions.

Juliet greatly resembles Antigone in recognizing what must be done regardless of the consequences, even if that is to no effect. Although they are in radically different situations, with Juliet acting as a revolutionary rather than as upholder of social mores, the two characters are equally uncompromising. Surely courage is a recognition of what one cannot change, refusing to betray one's dharma. This acceptance is not merely passive submission; at the same time it becomes an act of reckless abandon. The observation that one has no alternative is a confession of weakness which demands great strength of purpose. Giselle is entirely victimized, a creature of pathos; Juliet is a hero and a force to be reckoned with. Unlike Giselle, she never lies to herself. Though she looks like a young girl, she is ferocious and clear minded. Her movements should indicate this, for dance is an expressive art form, and the audience cannot be expected to guess Juliet's true nature. Above all she is uncompromising, following the example of Saint Paul rather than of Seneca, throwing caution to the winds.

The impulse to greatness which leads us to disregard danger must be motivated by an overwhelming belief that we are doing the right thing, whether it be an act of altruism, fulfilment of one's role in society or (as in Juliet's case) recognition of one's true self. It is not something to be done lightly. James Graham, Marquis of Montrose, celebrated this impulse (in males, at least) when he wrote:

He either fears his Fate too much,
Or his Deserts are small,
That puts it not unto the Touch,
To win or lose it all.

Juliet gambles and loses, but she never regrets her choice. Her life is short, but it is glorious.

As we watch this ballet, the music ringing in our ears expresses directly the emotions of the tiny figures on stage. Although they can be seen as puppets manipulated by fate, their riotous joy, ecstasy, fury and grief still belong to the characters themselves. **Romeo and Juliet** covers an immense canvas. With the breadth of its various perspectives, it ascends all possible heights and plumbs all possible depths. No ballet is more ambitious. These characters live life to the fullest extent. We are treated to the entire panorama. Presenting this in three hours is quite a feat. The score is gigantic: it conveys so much life, such a frenetic pace, such frenzy in its joy and sorrow, its gaiety and anger, its pride and its chilling fear, that it seems to court destruction. The action is too fiercely intense, rushing headlong toward the abyss. Because of time constraints, the ordinariness of every day is given less time than it occupies in our lives, and slow pacing is the only element missing from this monumental work, with the result that we are overwhelmed by its impact.

Both Juliet and Giselle reach the ultimate level of pain that they can bear to experience, but Juliet is a larger character. In fact, Juliet is portrayed as a whole person whom you might actually meet outside the context of the ballet. She has great force of action and her pain is an immense and terrible thing, while Giselle's is wistful, poignant, somehow insupportable because of her fragility and passivity. Giselle's gentle suffering is contained within her tiny body. Juliet, made of sterner stuff, has staked her fate on another, has forgotten herself, and we are less concerned for her ability to bear her wounds. We know she is prepared to die.

Some of the ballet's imperfections arise from flaws in Shakespeare's play. It seems ill knit compared to his later tragedies. First of all, it has two heroes who rarely meet. We follow Romeo through most of the first two acts, and only later do we intimately know the relative stranger, Juliet. Romeo's impulsiveness in killing Tybalt and even in swallowing poison might suggest a fatal flaw, but the same quality is a virtue in his love for Juliet. (I personally consider this inconsistency to be an asset.) Characters drift in and out of the story. Many are introduced but never become developed. Mercutio is actually eliminated in the second act, perhaps in compensation for his dominating presence.

The supporting characters are varied but seem flat. Their behaviour under duress surprises us because they are strangers. We have been given no information on what is happening in their lives, no clue by which to predict Lady Capulet's misery, her husband's possessiveness, her brother's belligerence, her nurse's duplicity, her confessor's timidity. Even the two main protagonists are a mystery to us where their relationships to others are concerned. We know them fully only as they reveal themselves to each other. Until the end of the second act, central relationships in Lady Capulet's life, and even in Romeo's, are unfamiliar to us. But then, perhaps these surprises are appropriate. After all, life is full of them. We know so little of what goes on in others' lives until a crisis emerges. **Romeo and Juliet** is full of untold stories.

And life includes shocking isolated incidents. We know very little about most of our acquaintances unless a crisis emerges, and our world refuses to wrap itself up into a single finished story. Art selects certain elements from the world and represents them in such a manner as to invoke responses associated with life experiences. Having suffered these experiences, we can glory in the benefits without having to relive the suffering. But Romeo and Juliet is a very large work, and I believe that the very untidiness and unpredictability of life are elements which have been deliberately included in it. The story's proximity to real life experiences is so disturbing that at times we lose the privilege of glorying in their benefits without paying the price. This ballet can get too close for comfort.

Prokofiev's music merges direct beauty and storytelling technique through its use of leitmotif, relating events specifically but with screaming strings and blaring brass. No choreography has ever succeeded in matching this accomplishment. In every version, pedestrian scenes propelling the plot forward are juxtaposed with pas de deux which directly express the lovers' passion through the pure beauty of their movement. Never do both methods manage to blend. The dancers walk through the acting scenes and soar in the love scenes. To date this problem has remained insurmountable.

There has been widespread criticism directed toward all choreographic treatments of Tybalt's death in Act II, in which his reluctance to die results in a lengthy struggle with ridiculous effect. Although it is definitely a fault to allow humour to undermine the drama of Tybalt's death, nevertheless I find that each time I see this scene I am less amused and more horrified, and I remember that life's most terrible events can be inadvertently funny from some perspectives. And watching **Romeo and Juliet** is like watching life. This is not a fragile ballet with rigid requirements regarding what is tasteful, and even a sojourn into absurdity can be absorbed into the panorama. Every facet of the human condition is welcome.

I have heard it said that all characters in the ballet seem flat except for Romeo and Juliet themselves. The two lovers tear themselves away from a backdrop which includes everyone else in the story. This is appropriate because they alone do not belong in their setting. They alone have no concern for traditions, social conventions or even their own safety. All others have proven themselves evil by opposing the real world of love in which Romeo and Juliet truly reside, a world whose vividness exposes the duplicity of all other characters, making them appear two dimensional by comparison.

The secondary roles seem to be glimpsed as in our lives we often catch a fleeting impression of others. There is no question of the fact that they lead lives of their own and that their concerns are important to them. Romeo and Juliet are not arrogant toward these people; they simply do not endorse their compromises. The friar is well meaning but half committed. Paris is a decent man who has not been told the truth because those who should tell him do not know it themselves. Expecting to be treated as he treats others, he is sadly wronged. Lady Capulet, in contrast to Lady Montague, is a haughty woman who shares her brother's misanthropy. In her affection for her brother and for her daughter she is secretly vulnerable, showering all her love on them. Her husband is defensive about his dysfunctional family and about his threatened position as traditional head of the household. Embarrassed by his wife's preference for her brother and by his daughter's rebellion, he bullies Juliet out of fear for his position and his family name. Lacking insight, he is unaware of his own motives.

Juliet's nurse deserves special consideration. Were it

not for her phlegmatic presence, one of life's commonest elements would be missing from the giant tapestry. It bothers her not at all that she is a source of constant amusement to everyone. The salt of the earth, and none too delicate in her tastes, she is not extraordinarily bright, not extraordinarily virtuous, and not extraordinarily wise, but unquestionably she is a dear old thing. She is not one to rise to any test of character, since unlike her charge she is a follower rather than a leader. She is not particularly courageous, and can even be a bit dishonest, but she is well intentioned and wants other people to be happy. She has the cheerful, conforming lack of scruples which would enable her to comfortably switch religions if this proved expedient, and this makes her the perfect foil for Juliet. At the same time, she has an instinctive knowledge that some things are wrong because she follows her heart rather than her mind. There is always a place in her ample bosom for any hurt thing. Warm hearted and generous, she cannot be dismissed as sentimental, courting pain self consciously with an ignorance of the real thing. She is not self conscious enough for that. Although she can easily forget her resolutions, her sympathy is genuine and unreflective. She is true to herself, and therein lies a spark of greatness —a greatness of which we are all capable.

Tybalt, on the other hand, is not merely compromising: he is truculent and nasty. Everyone except his sister hates him cordially. Again, note how the story of **Romeo and Juliet** is lifelike in every detail of character. How often have we observed no redeeming qualities in a person whom someone else finds mysteriously attractive? Probably Tybalt and his sister have been disliked from early childhood, and with good reason. This could be the secret of their mutual bond. One might be inclined to sympathize with them before becoming one of their victims. But unlike his sister, Tybalt has no secret affections. He harbours resentment over his unpopularity, but he nonetheless has earned it by being totally concerned with his own hurt feelings to the exclusion of everyone else's. He is a socially maladapted individual obsessed with his suspicion that others are laughing at him, because he never truly sees the world from anyone else's point of view. This makes him a perfect target for Mercutio, who is delighted to confirm the suspicions.

The three young blades were Shakespeare's invention. It was he who created the characters of Mercutio and Benvolio, borrowing only Mercutio's name from a character in Bandello's original narrative. The names were doubtless deliberately chosen to reflect the characters of the three friends: romantic, mercurial and benevolent. Whether they are more than friends is generally left open to speculation, except in Macmillan's version of the ballet. Benvolio does not seem to tag after his two more dashing companions, but instead regards himself as an mediating influence, trying to keep them out of trouble. He is a faithful and much needed friend, and it is he who smuggles Romeo away from the scene of Tybalt's death. It is sad that Friar Laurence does not entrust him with his message to Romeo the following day, for Benvolio is loyal and dependable. As for Mercutio, life is a lark to him. Lacking Romeo's sensibilities, he does not trouble himself with serious matters, and he meets the fate usual to characters of his reckless type. He is unaware of the pain which he is causing when he taunts the paranoid and hypersensitive Tybalt. He considers Romeo, the dreamer, subject to fits of madness which he dismisses as no fun. With bluff good humour he offends the whole world, and he gets away with it because everyone can see that he has no idea what effect he has. Everyone, that is, but Tybalt, who cannot recognize good humour because he has none.

And so for the first and last time, Mercutio's luck runs out, as one day it was bound to do.

I cannot say I entirely approve of Romeo. However, he is so handsome and charming that he is always forgiven his misdemeanors against everyone's better judgment. He is our great weakness, and he knows it. In particular he is the darling of all the womenfolk, doubtless thoroughly indulged by his mother. Macmillan, strong on personal touches of character, saves his wittiest moments for Romeo. This is a young man who possesses the charm that gets him the biggest piece of cake or the first place in line. He is debonair and mischievous, and it is not entirely his fault that so many people fall for him, though a good deal of responsibility does lie with him. He and Mercutio are the life of every party.

But there is more to Romeo than this. He is idealistic as well as devil-may-care. Until he meets Juliet his romantic affiliations are entirely self conscious and involve a false impression of himself as a constant and devoted lover. But his sudden infatuation with Juliet is a precious and beautiful thing. People who dismiss limerence are people who have no imagination. No, Romeo knows nothing whatsoever about Juliet. Yes, he is responding to her appearance. But whatever you may say about this young troublemaker, he has the soul of an artist who strives for what is pure and noble, and he truly intends to marry the beautiful girl whom he adores. He has the

capacity to become a responsible man and a truly
devoted husband, if married to the right woman.

On the other hand Romeo is impulsive, even
impetuous, and very highly strung. When in pain he
reacts instinctively and with unthinking anger. Both
lovers are happy to leap into their dangerous
situation, but Juliet does it with eyes open, fully aware
of the consequences, and she does not trust that if
she wants something enough she is bound to get her
way. Forethought is not Romeo's strong point, and
he rushes headlong into situations which bring about
his downfall. This is a young man who causes the
death of three people in twenty-four hours, not
including himself and Juliet. I am particularly appalled
that he has not considered how dangerous Tybalt
might be to his friend. Tybalt is not going to change
just because a Montague has married into the family.
Romeo is an untried youth, afraid of his own
impulses, and does not know (any more than we)
how brave he truly can be when not riding the wave
of his passions. In the face of Lady Capulet's alarming
and magnificent grief at her brother's death, Romeo
seems very young, very scared and very sorry. As he
gazes mutely at her in miserable bewilderment and
terror, I feel the urge to mother this boy. Like
everyone else, I have fallen for his charm.

Like Romeo, Juliet is not a 'flat' character. As I have
said, she is presented as someone you might meet in
real life, which is appropriate for a character from
what is basically a true story. Juliet's suffering recalls
our own as the godlike figures of **Swan Lake** cannot.
Her sexuality, her anger, and most of all her humour
prepare us for her grief. We suffer with her because
we have laughed with her. The play is full of lyric
poetry, but Prokofiev suggests no dewy young

maiden. His Juliet is a modern girl reflecting the revolutionary values of the time when Cranko and Macmillan created their versions of the ballet. She is a rebel, defiant and true to her convictions. After accepting a twentieth century ballet with a medieval setting we have no trouble embracing Juliet's modernity, and we see her as a teenager facing the dilemma which all young people in any time and place have had to endure.

Her creators have placed few stipulations upon her portrayal, leaving a great deal of choice to the individual performer, allowing each dancer to play herself as she truly is in real life. The wholeness of this character is unique in the ballet repertoire, which offers no other of such scope and complexity. The dancer is free to behave as she would in private life if confronted with Juliet's circumstances. This freedom to portray oneself fully, without censoring parts of one's character, makes the role of Juliet easy, in a sense. Since every dancer performs Juliet as herself, interpretations differ more than with any other role.

We must remember that Juliet is trapped in a position of powerlessness. Those of us who remember our teen years will find it easiest to relate to Juliet by calling to mind that time in our lives. The real Juliet was about seventeen, according to the true history of the couple written by Bandello. The conflicts in her life were similar to those which now confront younger adolescents, but we must remember that she had few hopes of eventual freedom and her situation resembled that of a modern thirteen year old. The assertiveness of Prokofiev's music is reflected in her body language; remember that young people's movements are calculated to make them appear older and more independent than they are. If Juliet were to 'act young' she would not be behaving like a teenager, and would not reach out to contemporary audiences.

We must remember also that Juliet is a Capulet. When she finds herself cornered she rises to the challenge, looking squarely at the truth and making her choice between Paris and the sleeping potion. When she defies her parents after being forced to dance with Paris in Act III Scene III, we suddenly see that she is no longer the young girl who stood aside from her formidable family when Romeo was challenged at the ball. From the moment she turns on her parents, we know that Juliet has the strength to take the path of her destiny, that she will go through with her plan and will accept whatever fate may come of it. She already has the potion, and while she becomes indecisive regarding precisely when she will drink it, she knows she has no choice but to take it that day. Juliet is as stubborn as every other member of her family, and she is not going back on her decision to drug herself. Marrying Paris is not an option for her. A certain muscularity conveys her inner strength. In real life appearances deceive, but appearances are the realm of the stage and Juliet's physical forcefulness is used here as a direct expression of her defiant spirit.

Romeo gets the turning point, but Juliet steals the show with the climax. The third act belongs to her. Facing her decision in solitude without Romeo's support, she becomes miraculously transformed into a woman before our eyes within the four walls of her bedchamber. She holds firmly to her love despite all urgings to betray all that is beautiful to her, to compromise, to follow the conventional path. Juliet has an unbending core of integrity. She makes active decisions with a will of her own. For while Giselle is a figure of pathos, Juliet is a hero.

Juliet is not preoccupied with herself. We do not find ourselves (as we do with Giselle) tortured by the suspense of wondering when catastrophe is going to befall her. Nor do we wonder whether and how she is going to bear it. Giselle's needs are uppermost in our minds because they assume that position in her own. We feel differently with Juliet because she grows out of the carefree, irresponsible girl we see at first. When she cannot avoid responsibility she emerges as a woman capable of looking squarely at her choices, unflinchingly making her decision. She does not spend time contemplating her vulnerability, and consequently it does not grow in her mind.

Juliet is a gambler. She plays her game to the full, and she loses. If given the opportunity for a second chance in the same circumstances she would do exactly the same thing again. And if that is how she feels about her love, then she is wise to gamble, and it is nobody's place to deny it. She knows what is important to her, and her decisions are made after weighing against it the sacrifices which have to be made. She does so impulsively because there has never been any question in her mind that her love is worth any price. If she loses Romeo then she has no desire to live anyway. And perhaps in gambling for her happiness she shows a wisdom which many of us have forgotten. She chooses to wager her life rather than to half live it. She knows her mind. Is she a fool to care about something so passionately that she is willing to win or lose all? Are humans meant for less than this? We should envy her such conviction. She is one of the few who are truly wise.

In thirty-six hours Juliet experiences enough to fill a

lifetime. Her cataclysmic decisions are in defence of a fledgling relationship with someone she has just met. The real Juliet had a longer marriage, but the play on which the ballet is based transforms her into a woman over a fly-by-night relationship. In the ballet Prokofiev's music provides the solution to this problem. If it says hers is a woman's grief, who are we to argue? As a rule I prefer poignancy over thunder. Quietly tearing down the walls to our hearts with a single touch —that is strength. But the score of **Romeo and Juliet** is truly effective in its extraversion. Of course, you have to work hard if you want to go the extravert route, but Prokofiev managed it. The audience sees a heroic metamorphosis and is reminded of how important it is to remain great despite all pressures to conform. Everyone emerges from the lesson a bigger person.

By nature Juliet is agitated, always poised at the height of awareness. We associate her intensity with her whole being, with every moment of her life. Even when Giselle is in a state of mental collapse, she is more passive than Juliet would be asleep. Juliet's arms do not have classical fluidity. Her hands are not dainty, and they betray her fierce strength. While Giselle's torso is static, Juliet's expresses her emotions with mighty upheavals influenced by modern dance, and she is capable of truly primal abdominal contractions. Her thin shoulders bend under their obligations and straighten proudly to accept them. Emphasis on the shoulders is deliberately intended to invoke the metaphor likening assumption of responsibility to taking a burden upon one's shoulders. Thus Juliet's stance illustrates her situation perfectly.

Her face is electrifyingly intense, quite unlike

Giselle's. Every muscle is taut. The eyes leap out from such a face, whose lines seem to revolve around their brightness. This effect can be achieved by closing the mouth to emphasize the chin, and by narrowing the corners of the eyes.

Except for the young girl in **Solitaire**, Juliet is the only character in any ballet whom we can imagine jumping off the proscenium and joining the audience. Her energy therefore must be sufficiently overwhelming for us to forget that classical ballet is a contrived and artificial way of moving. This is not difficult, and I will tell you why.

Dancers are trained athletes whose bodies have become accustomed to an artificial way of moving. In leisure moments you can catch a ballerina reclining with one foot around ear level and the other perfectly arched, encased in the armour of a pointe shoe which would cause excruciating pain to any ordinary citizen. In this peculiar position she might be smiling and conversing, her arms unconsciously moving in a manner which only years of training can produce. Outsiders to the world of dance cannot seem to understand that this has become second nature. But dancers live in a cloistered society where everyone knows that their amazing body language is entirely unselfconscious. Juliet could therefore join the audience intact: if she did, she would simply be a dancer. And precisely because they are less deliberate, this is one of the few ballets in which neoclassical western arm movements are preferable to Russian. Attention to detail is not a hallmark of Juliet's impulsive character, and in the best acting scenes her arms do not have classical beauty.

When her womanly resolve emerges in the third act,

we see how her body has developed. When treated like (or behaving like) a child, she shows us how lately she has crossed the threshold of puberty. And sometimes we see girl and woman together. But adolescents are like that. I shall elaborate upon this later.

The childlike enthusiasm which we see in Act I, Scene II should not be discarded for the rest of the ballet. One is expected in a work of art to introduce themes and to develop them toward a climax. Now, I realize that this singularly realistic ballet includes all factors which contribute to the complexity and un-expectedness of our not so simple lives, in which things do not fit smoothly into boxes and anything is possible. All factors, that is, except the slow and steady passage of time. But nevertheless, Juliet's youthful exuberance must be allowed to reveal itself intermittently. I emphasize that it must never be self conscious. I repeat, only adults try to look young. Teenagers want to look older than they are.

Likewise, the stubborn nature which comes into its own in Act III is suggested in her selfconscious decorum at the end of Act I, Scene II. It is more apparent when she is reluctantly led away from Romeo at the ball. Her pride and strength are hinted at as she joins the famous 'Pillow Dance'. She is appealingly shy, like a wild animal, yet for all her hesitation and in spite of the obvious attempt of a young girl to appear dignified at her debut, there is something about her which commands respect. She is every inch a Capulet. Her parents (as we know) are a formidable pair, especially her mother. There is something of Lady Capulet in Juliet's dismissal of her nurse, when the latter tries to interfere at the lovers' first meeting. It is quite clear who gives the orders, and in her few years Juliet must have learned that there are many ways to have her way with someone like her old nurse. And since Juliet is a tease, she may enjoy the witty choreography which Macmillan has provided for the Gavotte at the ball –perhaps even as much as Romeo, who has deliberately planned to finish the dance confronting her face to face.

The undulating repetition of two notes suggests the music of night insects at the beginning of the balcony scene, and the organ which we hear in the background for sixteen bars suggests the constant sound behind all sounds, perhaps of air beating against our eardrums, of which we will be aware if we sit very still in silence and listen. Prokofiev's music is so graphic as to become literal. Juliet hears a sound, looks for its source, searches again....

Those pulsating eight bars during which the lovers stand motionless, crossing the distance between them with their eyes as if to say, "You came, you came" – those eight bars attest to the power of that stillness upon which all movement is created. Those few seconds could be an eternity, and the universe one garden in Verona.

For the first time in his life, Romeo is overwhelmed and humbled by something greater than himself. I never could have imagined that I might be moved by the dropping of a cloak. But his is a cloak which trembles and pauses for a moment before slowly reaching the stage, like a living being, and Romeo sheds all his pretensions along with it, leaving him very young, very earnest, and very frightened.

It must be admitted that Macmillan has given us a Romeo and Juliet whose personal touches capture the essence of romantic love. The pregnant moment can hold no more and gives birth to a sudden flurry as Juliet descends, but before reaching each other she and Romeo hesitate. They face one another, breathless and afraid. Suddenly chilled by the breeze, they huddle together in their new shyness as they walk hesitantly forward, eyeing their feet. Exuberance overcomes Romeo, and Juliet watches with eyes blazing both in admiration and in excitement over their daring. She moves along the wall like a predator until overcome by a gentler ecstasy. And to the sound of a wind gathering she closes her eyes, throws back her head, opens her arms wide, and runs. While Cranko is the great master of pas de deux technique – and nobody knows so well how to intertwine two bodies in perfect harmony– nevertheless it is Macmillan's images which remain with me. The sight of Romeo lingering in the shadows after Juliet finally vanishes is forever imprinted on my mind.

I remember very well what it was to be a teenager, an adult forced into the role of child in a family run by other people. In Act III, Scene III, when Juliet remembers her love and her reason for taking the potion, we see a woman. And yet as soon as her father enters she reveals her conditioning to behave like a little sulking girl who has a nerve talking back to her 'superiors'. This is in reaction to her own self image as imposed by her perception of how her father sees her. We operate on the feedback we get from others even if we know it is wrong, and she is rendered ineffective by her father's preconceptions about her. Juliet's eyes are cast down in the obligatory deference of slave to master, unable to bear the sight of her reflection in his eyes.

Sartre wrote of this phenomenon, using Jean Genet

as an example –a reluctance to see oneself as an object to another person's consciousness. It is a common reaction to accusing stares from members of fashionable social groups, and this reaction persists even when the one with the downcast eyes knows that it is the accusor who really ought to be ashamed. The one with the downcast eyes is reacting not to any internalized belief in his or her own innocence, but merely to an awareness of the accusor's belief in his or her guilt. Sometimes, you can have a clear conscience because there is nothing in it. Such is the power of the Other, and only Juliet's deepest rage overcomes it. Even then, it does not succeed without a little rush of real surliness to push it over the edge, a side of Juliet which we have not seen before. She fixes upon her parents the unwavering, predatory gaze of the wolf. Now it is her conscience that is clear, and they are the objects of scrutiny. And in that moment, Juliet's defiance becomes the triumph of reality over appearance, of truth over lies, of love over social convention, and the fundamental conflicts of the story are resolved. It is the most important moment in the ballet.

I remember how, when I was a teenager, I sought refuge in my bedroom. I remember also how it was invaded. It is most appropriate that Juliet's key scene takes place in her bedroom. It is the only room in the house where an adolescent feels that she can freely be herself without being haunted by her history as a subordinate child. More than a room, it is a kingdom. It is a world. And her bed is her final haven. The bedroom is home to her, and it is here that we finally come to know her.

For this reason I shall spend some time concentrating on the original libretto for Juliet's bedroom scenes. In order to do this, it will be necessary to explain that Prokofiev's score consists entirely of a series of leitmotifs strung together and intertwined. In Cranko's version of the ballet, certain steps are used in the same way. In general, music is a law unto itself and is not intended to convey information as speech does. And for the most part I would say that explicit story telling demotes the art form. But when the story itself is moving, leitmotif derives its value as part of the whole work. I shall begin describing the action suggested by the music from the time Romeo has just left the bedchamber. I hope that any musicians reading this article will forgive my reducing bars to beats of twos or threes, an attempt to render the complex score more approachable to readers.

In Article #40 we have:
The nurse's theme, for 26 beats of 2. She enters to warn Juliet that her parents are approaching.
The nobles' theme from Act I, Scene III, for 12 beats of 3. Juliet's mother enters.
The theme from Juliet's first entry at the ball, for 19 beats of 3. This is the theme of an unattached girl soon to be married, which Juliet is no longer. Her mother tells her of the wedding plans.

In Article #41 we have:
The girlish theme from Act I, Scene II, for 30 beats of 2.
A proper temper tantrum ensues, or so her anger is seen. Juliet's love theme, expressing the passion that lives on when she has to face the world alone, for 13 beats of 2. Juliet's mother leaves her to think.
The theme from the 'Pillow Dance', indicating pride, power and family status, for 30 beats of 2. Juliet's father enters in a rage. It is on the 23rd beat that

Juliet collapses in exhausted tears. As the music
subsides, her father gives up and leaves.

In Article #42 we have:
After a pause, the overture theme asking us why this
should ever happen, for 20 beats of 3. The thin sound
of violins emphasizes the pathos of Juliet's situation.
In at least one version Juliet gazes through her
window overlooking the garden. Romeo is out there
somewhere.

In Article #43 we have:
The parting love theme, for 21 beats of 3. Juliet is not
the pathetic type. She decides to visit Friar Laurence.

In Article #44 we have:
Juliet's entry to Friar Laurence (3 beats), and the
marriage theme (2 beats) as she agitatedly pleads for
his help.
The balcony scene theme, as he thinks (3 beats), then
the marriage theme again (4 beats) as he calms her,
and the balcony scene theme (2 beats).
Then our first introduction to Juliet's waiting theme
(2 beats) as he explains the purpose of the sleeping
potion.
In all, 16 beats of 2.
Then we have the waiting theme, for 19 beats of 2.
Juliet returns to her bedchamber. She suddenly
succumbs to her dread.
A theme from the marriage scene, for 6 beats of 2.
Juliet is worried, but on the last 2 beats remembers
again how dear Romeo is to her.

In Article #45 we have:
The balcony scene theme, for 8 beats of 2. Juliet
resolves that nothing in the world matters but the
greatness which she has momentarily forgotten.

An intermediary 2 beats of 2.
The overture theme, for 3 beats of 3, summing up
Juliet's resolution.

In Article #46 we have:
The 'Pillow Dance' theme, for 6 beats of 2. Lord and
Lady Capulet enter with Paris, ready to force Juliet's
compliance. Juliet surveys them disdainfully.
The overture theme, for 10 beats of 3. In Macmillan's
version Juliet runs to her mother. After all, she has
just made a frightening decision for a young girl. In
addition, she knows she may never see her mother
again. A portion of the parting love theme finishes
this section.
The theme to which Juliet danced with Paris at the
ball, for 10 beats of 3. Juliet consents to dance with
Paris.
Then, for 5 beats of 3 she tries to push him away,
unsuccessfully, unable to bear his touch.
Agonized, she falls to the floor, for 4 beats of 2, and
he lets go.
The theme resumes for 8 beats of 3 as Juliet frigidly
allows herself to be manipulated by Paris.
Obviously however, for 7 beats of 2 she is quite
disgusted with everybody, and the three leave her
alone for fear of causing more trouble. They have no
idea what to do with her in this new mood. She gives
them nothing to fight and yet there is clearly
something wrong. They decide to go while things are
quiet and it is possible for everyone to assume that
she is complying with their wishes. If this keeps up
she might just walk through the wedding ceremony,
as long as nobody breathes.

In Article #47 we have:
4 single beats. Juliet takes the potion, and violently
reacts to her impulsive gesture.

The waiting theme, for 22 beats of 2. It has
happened, and the waiting has started.
The balcony scene theme, for 7 beats of 2, as she
remembers her love.
The first effect of the potion is felt, for 3 beats of 2.
There follows the waiting theme, for 8 beats of 2.
Juliet's love theme, as in Article #41. She sits in the
middle of the bed, waiting. An ominous theme
employing what I call the 'death chord', for 8 beats of
2, used here to indicate the passage of time as Juliet
loses consciousness. In Cranko's version, the lights
fade for 2 or 3 beats, after which we see Juliet lying
unconscious, her left arm outstretched to where
Romeo has lain (one of Cranko's visual leitmotifs).

The contrast between girl and woman is central to
these scenes. When Juliet is bullied by her father's
anger at his own helplessness, she tries to curl up and
withdraw, while he deliberately tries to whip up his
adrenalin in support of the wife who has just
disgraced him in public.

Article #43 is generally used for a scene change, but it
is also a glorious opportunity to emphasize Juliet's
heroism as she resolves not to give up her struggle. A
tiny but determined figure in the middle of a chaotic
firmament, she defies her fate. As the music subsides
and we see Friar Laurence's cell, a bedraggled little
figure enters, shivering and forlorn. The power of this
ballet lies in the clarity of its conflicts. We witness a
constant struggle, and are made to see every minute
of the process. Juliet loses her battle against fate, but
she wins the struggle to free her soul. This is only one
of the sequences when we see her fight, grow tired,
gather her strength, and fight again.

The original Russian version emphasises a heavenly

moment of wistful remembrance at the end of Article #44. As Juliet walks downstage, her face has a shining beauty and her body an unsurpassed womanliness. And just as suddenly they seem to alter as her parents enter. Her contempt is made to appear like a foolish whim, even though we know how fully justified it is. She slips into her accustomed role in the family, and although the dignity in her performance is real, she fails to convey it to her parents.

Greatness provides no guarantee that anyone will be impressed. Any degree of insensitivity is possible. The unthinkable can happen, if people are just not aware of what is going on. Nobody comes down from the sky with thunderbolts, declaring that this cannot happen. History's atrocities have taught us that. And no matter what has happened to Juliet, her parents see her as nothing more than a petulant child. They have long been conditioned to do this, and so has Juliet. Though fortified by her memories of Romeo, she shrinks before people who are smaller than she, feeling that she has a nerve to impudently defy her parents.

But do not forget that, as I have remarked before, Juliet is a Capulet. However subdued her stand against her parents, it is stubbornly defiant. Whatever they choose to make of it, the stand is not temporary. She might make use of her deliciously mocking sense of humour as she dances with Paris. The lengthy introduction to this dance allows plenty of time for this. Her very passivity and reserve are a tongue in cheek comment upon the situation. My guess is that she cannot resist a half smile and a contemptuous glance through lowered eyelashes, even though her body is quivering with tension at her unpleasant proximity to Paris.

After she screams in agony at his unwelcome touch, she picks herself up and resumes as if in a trance. The conditioning is gone. Nothing they may think can affect her now. As she breaks off, there is a dangerous hint of real brutality which even her parents cannot fail to notice. The beast which resides in each of us has finally come out. The three intruders silently withdraw, instinctively protecting themselves by pretending that they have seen nothing, but beating a swift retreat.

A steady, dull stare through slightly narrowed eyes in a lowered face is a standard message of aggression. Bringing the lower jaw forward alters the entire face, especially if the jaw is a little to one side so that the teeth do not quite mesh. It is not a pretty look. Why, for a second there Juliet looks like Uncle Tybalt.

Dear Uncle Tybalt. And what a lovely family the Capulets are. A man of the Catholic Church, no less, is afraid to tell them that he has married their daughter to an enemy, leading me to think that the real Friar Laurence had no real hope of reconciling the families, and merely felt sorry for two victims of circumstance. Everyone involved in the conspiracy agrees that the couple will be able to elope only if the Capulet family believes Juliet to be dead. We can assume that otherwise Capulet henchmen will be all over the countryside long before Romeo can get away.

Prokofiev uses a great deal of suggestive imagery, such as the resemblance of the waiting theme to a clock, and the faint rattle of cymbals to signify death. When one of these audial images occurs, this does not mean that what it signifies is physically present. Sometimes it indicates what is in the mind of a character onstage, and sometimes it is a commentary on something of which the characters are unaware, but is intended to be informative. The death chord in Article #47 is an example of the latter. Obviously Juliet is not dead, but it is a neat piece of fore-shadowing.

Macmillan's version of the final scene includes a portcullis whose lowering seals in the tomb, emphasizing the trap into which the lovers have been heading and the irrevocability of their doom. In desperation, Romeo hacks at the corpse of the already dead Paris as the portcullis closes behind him. Crazed with grief, he stabs erratically at the body. The presence of Paris at Juliet's tomb must seem to him a sacrilege. Macmillan makes the most of the contrast between his frenzied movements and the slow, inexorable lowering of the heavy gate.

Consider what Juliet awakens to see: a haunted tomb, sealed until the next death in the family, with only one unreliable person knowing that she is alive in there. The least imaginative of us would contemplate suicide with the prospect which lies before Juliet — slow death by starvation in a dank tomb, surrounded by rotting bodies. The portcullis is an effective dramatic element.

The musical basis for Article #51 is the fate theme, which has previously occurred along with Juliet's waiting theme. The grinding end of Article #52 is a modification of this. The basis for the rest of Article #52 is the theme of Juliet's love first noted here in Article #41. It is introduced in a devastatingly effective way, rising like a dawn as Juliet moves happily in her sleep, dreaming that she is beside Romeo. Her hand reaches out to him, and this awakens her. Alarmed at her surroundings, she runs to the nearest thing she sees (what remains of Paris) and recoils when she finds that he is dead. She runs away again, toward stage right, and sees Romeo.

"You came," she thinks, believing him to be asleep, and fondly gazes with devotion at her love who so winningly slumbers by her bier, waiting to take her away. Tenderly she approaches and kneels beside him, her head inclined to see his face. The music

swings, as in the rocking movements of deep mourning, and Juliet's movement should echo this as she takes Romeo into her arms. We should see her face change above his corpse as she realizes the truth, and she is the kind of person who clings more tightly when shocked, not the type who drops what she is holding. Capulets do not let go easily. She remembers something which can take her out of this world, and runs over to the dagger which has killed Paris.

Although in every version of the ballet Juliet stares at the weapon with which she is about to end her life, it is my opinion that this is unnatural. Suicide is an impulsive act, and stabbing oneself is one of the most difficult ways to do it. Also, Juliet has no reason to hesitate.

When she falls to her knees, the balcony scene theme is briefly, wistfully recalled, a last hint of tender beauty before the music grinds into an exhausted dirge. She is sick, alone and dying. On its knees, her body caves in so that her forehead is hidden. Some force makes her want to die beside her love. She is terrible to see, dragging across the floor. One thought seems to pervade her blurred mind, an illogical force of will moving what is almost a corpse. She succeeds in getting to the bier, and leans over to pull Romeo up, feebly tugging at his arm. But her great will is overcome and she is defeated. The world is empty, and she screams silently, rolling slowly onto her back.

There is no apotheosis in this ballet. Tchiakovsky's music provides apotheosis, and Shakespeare's play has at least a moral statement at the end. But Prokofiev actually gives us some idea of what death is really like —the overwhelming sickness, the paralyzing terror, the horror of flesh that is not adequate to support life. We usually find that art lets us have everything our way, giving us a glimpse of greatness without requiring that we actually experience the circumstances in which it is achieved. We can revisit memories for which the spirit yearns without paying a price. With **Romeo and Juliet**, I sometimes find that too much is delivered. This mighty panorama of life ends with the physical degradation of rotting flesh, the absence of life, and no hope of heaven. The knife is twisted inside us. We have no cathartic experience. Instead we are treated to a vision of the reality which accompanies death, the reality of horrible sickness.

But still the gallantry and the courage stay in my mind, the memory of Juliet fiercely defying a foe stronger than herself. And of Romeo standing alone in that first night, outside Juliet's balcony after she is gone.

A WEALTH OF MASTERPIECES

You may recall my comment that in **Romeo and Juliet** the beauty of balletic movement and the meaning of the characters' experience never seem to join together. Antony Tudor has mastered the art of merging the two. He does not merely express the latter by means of the former, though figures swirl around his central characters, nameless muses directly personifying their feelings. Tudor's genius lies in this, that he alone of all in his field has achieved mastery in wedding two kinds of physical expression.

No other choreographer is capable of producing a work as passionate and yet as controlled and under-stated as **Lilac Garden**. The effect of this ballet is created by our understanding of the characters' situations as they betray their emotions by means of only the subtlest nuances. Yet this effect is underlined and intensified by the swirling figures which become outward manifestations of the characters' inner torment. Tudor works on two levels with consummate ease. He recognizes the power of control, its sensitizing effect, the fact that volumes can be communicated by one look or by a tiny gesture more effectively than any direct, exaggerated expression of emotion. Yet he is capable of employing at the same time that very expression itself, athletic and extroverted, extending to the technical limits of the art of dance. I can think of no other choreographer who has simultaneously adopted both approaches, which are merely alternated in all versions of Prokofiev's **Romeo and Juliet**.

Caroline's narrow mindedness in no way diminishes the pathos of this perfect jewel of the ballet repertoire. Her pride is responsible for the understatement which imbues her every gesture with taut intensity. The complex detail of the interplay between the four main characters inspires the same enduring interest as a fine string quartet, forever offering its interpreters the opportunity to add a subtle touch here or there. Their very containment increases the pressure of the protagonists' emotions, betrayed by only the smallest gestures, while behind and around them contrasting figures echo what is really happening. And more —they express directly the feelings of the main characters, giving physical form to their torment.

During **Scheherezade** also, a certain control in Zobeide's gestures adds to the intensity of the ballet's effect. But here is a character in a different situation. Zobeide has not failed to consider all her options. She is physically enslaved and her containment is duplicitous. This woman can imagine herself in another situation, and would have swiftly escaped Caroline's garden.

The pride with which she controls her movement is tinged with contempt and hatred. She is mistress as well as slave, and both she and her master are fully aware of the fact. Conversely, she is slave as well as mistress to her secret lover, and there is in her both great strength and great weakness. The world in which she lives allows only power based relationships. The eunuch orders his assistants but looks to her for guidance, yet her power is not real – except over her lover, whom she releases from his cell periodically. That power is more attractive than influence over her master. She and the eunuch are in the middle of a power structure which is brilliantly portrayed, each character in the ballet possessing a point of view from which his or her actions appear justifiable. **Scheherezade** is first and foremost a treatise on slavery, the situations which arise from it, the complex relationship between master and slave, the hierarchies among slaves, and the intolerable damage this power play must inevitably cause.

The world of **Sleeping Beauty** is in contrast gentler and more gracious than ours, a world in which even the villain is beautiful. This is a childhood dream seen from the perspective of age, so that it delights the child in us without offending the adult. It cannot be dismissed as juvenile fare. Here is entertainment at its most refined, with just the faintest touch of greatness, enough real feeling to elevate it to the status of art.

Aurora's movements are intrinsically exciting. There is an exquisite tension particularly to the tiny developpés in her Act III solo, a conflict between thrusting and restraining forces which result in a slight pause before each extension, creating the impression that she is going to be behind the music, while she always (fascinatingly) manages to keep time. Although this tension is less evident at other times, it characterizes all her movements, conveying an impression of delicacy. Each of those marvellous sequences of 'pinwheel' bourrees, turning ecstatically at the end of the Rose Adagio, ends at a peak with Aurora's extended arm poised for a moment before beginning the next sequence. Similarly, her arm pauses with a curl of the wrist for a split second, before graciously accepting the outstretched hands offered her in the Rose Adagio and in both her pas de deux. There is even a moment of hovering before her graceful collapse after pricking her finger.

The sense of timing required to master such roles seems to be inherited. One is born with the gift for not just walking straight through a sequence, or one misses the boat. A similar talent is required to perform the Snow Scene pas de deux from **Nutcracker**, a thing of shimmering beauty. I was raised on a version in which the ballerina slowly walks forward to greet her prince for eight bars. There must be hesitation, especially if it is Clara who steps forward, for the best productions of **Nutcracker** acknowledge that it is a young girl's initiation into the world of adulthood, with the threatening spectre of a sexual relationship into which she is being gently introduced. She proceeds as follows:

bar 1 –Step forward onto the right foot;
bar 2 –Slowly wave the right hand overhead;
bar 3 –Step forward onto the left foot;
bar 4 –Slowly wave the left hand overhead
(incomplete movement);
bar 5 –Complete the wave on the first two beats, and
step forward on the third;
bar 6 –Take four eighth-note steps and on the
remaining quarter-note bring your right foot behind
you and face the prince
bar 7 –Curve the right arm toward you on the first
beat with neck arched forward, and raise it overhead
on the second and third;
bar 8 –Plié on your left leg for two beats, recovering
on the third.

Such awareness of timing is required also in that glorious wedding cake of a pas de deux which climaxes the third act of **Sleeping Beauty**. A winsome touch provided by the oboe adds a certain tenderness expressed in the solicitous manner of Aurora's prince, whose gallant and touching concern for his princess is graciously appreciated. Aurora, like Clara, is being initiated into a sexual relationship, but she is less vulnerable and more prepared.

In the area of interpretation known as character portrayal, Aurora is usually considered to be a narrow role, yet there is more to her than meets the eye. Endowed with beauty, poise and grace, with energetic generosity of spirit and a delicious sense of humour, with an understandable aura of well-being, with true musicality and with sparkling intelligence and charisma, she is blessed with five out of six thoughtfully chosen gifts from supernatural sources. She has grown up to be pristine, gracious and cultured, and doubtless has high standards of conduct.

Aurora's only flaw (and a charming one) is a slight disposition toward impulsiveness. She teases her courtiers by dancing with the spindle she has discovered, laughing at their horror. She is well matched by her dashing, playful prince, whose sense of fun equals her own as he enters the deserted palace. The intensity of Aurora's facial expression, except when she is actually laughing, is achieved by means of three basic movements. One is a smile which is stretched over an almost entirely closed mouth, giving the impression that she has high cheekbones. The second is a slight narrowing of the eyes with a direct gaze, suggesting intelligence and good humour. The third is an arching of the eyebrows, when she is amused. This charming being has missed only one important asset, the traditional gift symbolized by the lilac —the attribute of wisdom. No wonder she promptly marries the first man who kisses her.

Most of **Sleeping Beauty** is abstract dancing, and a far cry from the surrealism of twentieth century dramatic ballets. It is odd that after Balanchine created his first plotless ballets, retellings of detailed stories became quite popular. Sets were movable walls and the ballerinas wore street clothes over pink tights and pointe shoes. The intention was to suggest an environment rather than to represent it explicitly. Although this tradition became overused, its dreamlike effect is entirely appropriate in **Pillar of Fire**, during which the passion of the central character seems to have an almost telekinetic effect.

Fancy Free is one ballet in which the sets clearly reflect the characters' mood. They have been painted deliberately to represent a view of Manhattan as seen by a tipsy sailor enjoying shore leave. The buildings float, the bar has no door, and a lamp post is off balance. I am reminded of Picasso's remark: "I paint things not as I see them, but as they really are". The sets do not represent stone and concrete buildings in whose existence we agree to believe. They represent a subjective experience which is indisputably real to someone in a jolly mood. They illustrate the genuine qualities of ebullience, effervescence and good humour.

The decor for **Petruschka** also is vital to an understanding of the work as a whole in which two worlds coexist, a veneer of mundanity and the terrifying reality which it hides. But in **Petruschka**, the story, choreography and music also were created on these two levels along with the decor, making **Petruschka** the most thoroughly integrated of theatrical experiences, a great collaboration in which all elements equally serve the same muse.

It is possible to discover the truth about what is really going on simply by listening. The music gives it away. A fateful chord serves to connect scenes, providing continuity and underlining the meaning behind the action on stage. In addition, it acts as a chorus commenting upon the inevitability of the actions unfolding in the lives of the tiny unsuspecting creatures of the story. The characters onstage act separately from this sound, which is for our ears only. The string section is innocent enough, but its continuity is interrupted by frighteningly ill-suited brass instruments playing discordantly, as if the real world were breaking through the facade. The disharmony is indicative of the story's characters, each of whom has a selfish agenda at odds with the world as a whole. Musical themes appear and disappear, creating a scattered effect, as of many separate projects which never come together but die shortly after their birth, like the doomed souls in the story, who go their wilful ways in ignorance of the universal plan, only to die.

The colours in the ballet are oppressive. At the fair everything is too bright and gaudy, leading one to suspect that something is being hidden. We are warned of this by a sinister drop curtain depicting evil spirits flying above the fairground —at night, when the sun fails to illuminate all those distracting colours. The darkness of the drop curtain and of Petruschka's cell are even more oppressive than the fair, perhaps the more so because we know they represent the truth. The stars on the cell walls indicate the puppet's budding soul, but the sombre colour makes us feel trapped. The Moor's cell is another gaudy façade made up of simple colours to please those who are fooled by them.

Petruschka is often described as a puppet with a soul, but indeed all three puppets have consciousness. It is just not highly developed. And neither is the consciousness of the townsfolk, who do not see that the puppets reflect themselves, undeveloped beings subjected to karmic manipulation. Although the townsfolk are shocked by Petruschka's murder they can easily be fooled by appearances, and therefore become convinced that he has never been more than a stuffed doll. They fail to notice the suffering in front of their eyes, as long as it is masked by a thin facade. It is significant that they shrink from a performer in a devil's mask, while the real danger of a chained bear is ignored. The bear's movements are loose, as are Petruschka's. The other puppets move stiffly. So do the townsfolk, who look not unlike puppets themselves as they huddle in small groups whose rhythms fail to work with others. Like the puppets, they are manipulated by an evil force, and the puppet show is the town square in microcosm, which of course they fail to see.

Petruschka speaks to the human condition more than any other ballet. Of the three puppets, only one has a chance at salvation. When he is murdered, his appearance above the puppet theatre indicates that the promise is being fulfilled. But in order to receive the gift, now that he is free, like the few humans who have paid their karmic debt he must purge himself of the earthly impulses which will otherwise hold him back, and turn his back on evil. This he fails to do. He repeats the mistake made in the Garden of Eden. Instead of transcending, he succumbs to a tempting opportunity to taunt his tormentor, and loses his chance at eternity.

Carnaval shares with **Petruschka** the benefit of Diaghileff's genius for bringing various talents together. In his golden age, all elements of production were equal. Fragile as gossamer, ambiguously happy and sad at the same time, **Carnaval** must be performed with care. The figure of Pierrot is a far cry from the starkly symbolic Petruschka. Nothing is distinctly stated in **Carnaval**. It is even more difficult to master than the notoriously subtle **Les Sylphides**.

One of the first plotless ballets, **Les Sylphides** primarily suggests a mood. It stands somewhere in the middle, successor to numerous story ballets but predecessor to **Apollo**.

Les Sylphides can best be described as a series of sighs. Each inward breath is a priceless treasure, and the whole creation is as ephemeral as one respiration, so that when it is over and the spell is broken, one wonders whether it was a dream. Wistful and dreamlike, passing all too soon and leaving no trace, it is unbearable —yet we do not know why. Like a lost memory of moonlit nights from long ago, it has a profound yet elusive meaning, evoking a nostalgia for something we barely remember, something too beautiful to last.

The main problem in performing this work is the fact that the entire corps de ballet must understand it, and that is a tall order. All too often the dancers are carefully instructed not to smile, and in some of their arrangements they look positively nauseous, with the result that the heady atmosphere is turned into something miserable. I hate to think what they might be huddling over in some of their formations. Whatever happened to that wonderful smile that isn't a smile, the hallmark of the Romantic ballerina? As with **Giselle**, if you truly understand this ballet you need not worry about overstepping the mark of good taste. The spirit that moves you will not allow such a transgression.

By the way, that borne-on-the-breeze effect is achieved with a lot of small, quick steps which have no influence on the upper body. It is very effective to sway the upper body with a gentle whiplash effect of the arms, but this must be independent of lower body movement. It is a style peculiar to the Romantic era of **Giselle** and **La Sylphide**, to which this ballet pays homage.

La Sylphide, of course, possesses the magical smile. Hers is something more than Aurora's teasing charm. The eyes of the sylph are dark pools, unfathomable. To look into them is to experience the eerie impression of being drawn in uncontrollably. The mystery of those eyes may be due to the fact that there is nothing in them to disclose after all, nothing there to understand, no depths to fathom —only a voracious vacuum, and James dies for an illusion. However, I hold the opposite view.

Certainly he dies for an ideal of physical beauty, and should have settled for a real woman who, while less, would also have been more. But the special quality which seduces James is akin to what we yearn for in **Les Sylphides**, something which we can never quite capture.

La Sylphide is a perfect being, but she is a perfect being because she is limited, a creature without a soul. I think that the sylph's eyes draw us as the quest for knowledge draws us, without end, in a universe which is infinite. We can gaze forever and never reach the limit. This is a fact which we must accept with dignity.

The New Testament teaches us that we must keep trying for perfection, however unattainable it may be. But perhaps we are meant to do this by being more human, not by committing the original sin of trying to be something else. The goal is to be achieved by touching each other's hearts, not by deserting those who trust us and abusing those we find unattractive.

It is significant that James destroys the perfection he loves when he tries to possess her, when he tries to bring her into his own realm instead of accepting the fact that she will always elude him. And in so doing he also brings about his own ruin. It is a fact of life that as soon as we possess an ideal it ceases to be an ideal, but people are not things to be desired, they are beings to be loved. Our concern for how they feel should eclipse our disappointment at their imperfections.

We must not take literally our interpretations of ballets from this era. James does not imagine a perfect being who desires him any more than Giselle seeks revenge upon Albrecht. But the story of **La Sylphide** opens our minds to the limits of perfection just as the story of **Giselle** opens our minds to the psychology of a jilted lover.

Of course it is only when James insults an old woman from a defeated people that he seals his fate, displaying an arrogance that goes hand in hand with wanting more than he can have. Thus **La Sylphide** is a morality tale with a flawed male character as its pivotal central figure, precursor to that other great morality tale, **Swan Lake**.

In **Swan Lake** the romantic hero has become an allegorical figure. His story is equally cautionary, but unlike James, he is not a mortal man yearning for a symbol. He is a symbol himself, a symbol of manhood trying to be virtuous to women, and his attraction to the symbol of womanhood, Odette, becomes appropriate. The issue has now become his failure to distinguish spiritual from physical beauty, the flaw in male psychology which dooms him to failure.

The choreography of **Swan Lake** is more flowing than that of most ballets its age, at least in the 'white' acts for which Ivanov was responsible. Since Petipa choreographed the third act, it is not surprising that Odile's movements differ in style from Odette's. The accepted interpretation of the dual female role stresses the contrast between Odette's extended line and Odile's hard glitter.

However, since the original staging of **Swan Lake** was a failure and current productions are derived from the later Sergeyev version, perhaps we should admit that authenticity is not what we are striving for in this ballet. All productions that we see nowadays are neoclassical and are firmly entrenched in the twentieth century. A nineteenth century production would simply not be tolerated.

Sleeping Beauty was the ultimate that could be done with Petipa's classicism, but **Swan Lake** always transcended its boundaries. During an age of entertainment it raised its rebellious head with images of black crags, chill winds and shimmering waters hiding unspeakable tragedy, and from the very beginning attempts were made to tame it, even insertions of lesser music into its titanic symphonic score. In 1877 **Swan Lake** was an anachronism. Although unready, it belonged in the twentieth century.

Swan Lake is an allegory. It is the story of man, of his folly and of the price woman has to pay for it – and in the end it is the story of his ultimate worth. The characters are not individuals, they are symbols. Since it is wholly appropriate to update the interpretation of roles in this ballet, there is no reason to portray the virgin and the whore, which has never been anything more an excuse for rape. If Odile is seen solely from a man's point of view, the audience will see no more than Siegfried does. We are not merely looking at what one character perceives in this ballet. We are viewing the story of man from a godlike perspective.

Odile does not balance Odette. She is missing the true womanliness which Odette possesses, lacking her nobility of spirit. Her sexual languor is identical to Odette's, and it is this which blinds Siegfried to the fact that there is no tenderness behind it. With a fine dramatic irony, she can disguise her lack of finer feeling by exhibiting her exultation in deceiving him, which he will interpret as a feeling of triumph that she has persuaded Rothbart to let her attend the ball. She can look right into his eyes and still fool him.

Both Odette and Odile are voluptuous, with the alluring remoteness which comes of being female and therefore self-contained. But Odile's focus is on herself, while Odette is totally self-sacrificing toward her lover, all the while remaining fiercely protective of her flock –vulnerable and formidable at the same time, with the strengths and weaknesses of a woman. It is delicious to compare the two roles because many of Odile's movements are stylistically identical to Odette's. Her positioning before her Act III solo echoes the beginning of the Act II adagio. Its feigned modesty is a parody of Odette's fear during the first encounter.

The undulations of the Act II adagio express the conflicting urges toward flight and toward consummation, seeking to escape her lover and yet yearning for his touch. Together at first, tentatively exploring each other, the dancers break into their supported developés, the sequences of six hops and a lift over Siegfried's head between two lines of swans, and the following repetition three times of a fifth position and step into a rather wild attitude with a pirouette en dehors. It is after Odette runs to the corner following these attempts at flight, when Siegfried gives up hope that she will ever accept him, that the miraculous happens. He has touched her heart, and she comes to him at last.

Counterpoint is essential to her approach, before she leans over his bowed back to touch his shoulder and transform him with her love. The steps do not match the rhythm of the music. Essentially the music consists of four triplets, and the steps fall on the first note of the first, the first and third of the second, the second of the third and the first and third of the fourth.

Similarly, counterpoint is essential to the heroic finale. Odette beats her wings unevenly. Her entire torso strains with the wavelike movement. One wing brushes her hip and she leans to that side. While still leaning, she turns the other way with an abdominal contraction, bringing the other arm down. Both arms swing powerfully upward together, and the torso straightens from the opposing inclination and turn into a climactic lift. This circular movement belongs to the passionate dance forms of the twentieth century, a movement of the torso obeying primal laws. Indeed, both Odette and Odile are moved by contractions and releases of the Graham technique,

with limbs following like willow branches in the wind, a whiplash with every transition.

There are times when it is appropriate to move exactly in the rhythm of the music, particularly during the second act adagio. This is a study in breaking apart and coming together. Counterpoint is more often required during moments of bonding and syncopation in moments of separation. The tension between the two forces is endlessly fascinating. Never are music and movement more perfectly wed than during six bars of the opening section:

bar 1 –Posé in arabesque;
bar 2 –Turn en dehors toward the extended leg as it withdraws into retiré;
bar 3 –Extension of the leg, brush through a fifth position, retiré;
bar 4 –Extension of the leg in a developpé forward, one arm brushing over the leg, then the other;
bar 5 –Both arms extending upward, suspended;
bar 6 –Fall back onto Siegfried's arm.

The movements of the third and fourth bars are rhythmically matched to the score with three distinct movements in each bar, and for that brief space of time we see the music and hear the dance. The Act II adagio is the pinnacle of all that classical ballet has achieved, wedding music and movement in flawless perfection.

The Dying Swan is a symbol of all that is gentle and shining and beautiful. In three minutes she tells us all that matters in the world. It can never be told enough.

Pavlova reportedly was dissatisfied with the film which survives of her performance. Doubtless she knew that the camera should be at a distance, since the work was created for stage production, passion seen from afar. But however it was filmed, it was still a Pavlova performance as no one else could do it, a tiny fluttering creature valiantly and hopelessly struggling for its last breath. Imagine sitting in evening dress and watching the death throes of something so proud and courageous. And feeling removed, helpless. It is terrible to see the departure of an indomitable spirit, and as species disappear from the planet reality begins to imitate art.

Nevertheless, I am not among those who maintain that **The Dying Swan** should have died with Pavlova. Though no one will be able to duplicate what she was able to accomplish, I believe that other interpretations of the role are possible, emphasizing her gentleness and forgiveness rather than her heroism, the nobility rather than the indomitability of her spirit. This creature has harmed no-one. She has never done anything but bring joy and faith to everyone who has seen her. Yet now she must die, and somebody lives who has killed her. She does not understand why this crime has been committed, but she is not angry. This Dying Swan resigns herself to death with a generosity which makes us grieve all the more and ask ourselves why this terrible thing has been allowed to happen. It is a good question, and one which T.S. Eliot addressed when he wrote:

> ...I am moved by fancies that are curled
> Around these images, and cling:
> The notion of some infinitely gentle
> Infinitely suffering thing.
>
> Wipe your hand across your mouth and
> laugh....

For you are living at the end of the world.

Remarkably similar and yet utterly different in appearance, **Rite of Spring** is a study in fear and its relationship to our perception of time. Like **The Dying Swan**, it could go on forever and yet comes to a close at its own pace. We seem suspended in time when we are facing something terrible. That which we fear approaches too fast, and yet we can say that every moment is an eternity.

The Chosen One is terrified, but she is also resigned. Her mind knows no alternatives to her fate. She never questions what she dreads. She would not welcome a rescuer, for she believes that the survival of her people depends upon her sacrifice, and she is driven internally much as dancers are driven internally to endure pain for the sake of their art.

The inevitability of her execution is vital to the effect of the work. Most of the ballet is a ritual process leading to this event, and the action is contained within ritual because the people who perform it are not decision makers. A ritual follows its own course. It must be completed in its entirety, but it must be completed. Therefore it is hard to hurry a ritual, but it is also hard to slow it down. The Chosen One might well feel that her limbs are not her own, that she is floating above her body and it is moving of its own accord in the prescribed manner. In fact, the role can be performed as though she is disjointed. Only her face, neck and chest betray her fear by remaining tense and motionless, with the rest of her body in a frenzied whirl. She appears to be living on two levels, as one does when death is near, floating above her body in stunned agony while it does what it has to do.

Time seems to stand still also in **Afternoon of a Faun**, Jerome Robbins' study of adolescence. A single ephemeral moment is crystallized, a time and place separated from the rest of life for us to remember, like a painting by Vermeer in which everything is priceless and objects are suspended in a space which we see with new, appreciative eyes. This short work recaptures a pregnant, hushed and elusive moment in our lives which is all too easily forgotten, a moment when the world is new and we are far too aware of it.

An almost intolerable sensitivity is required of the performers. First, however, they must understand the stage in life which is being depicted. This should not be hard, since most of us have experienced the agony of adolescent courtship. As in the original **L'Apres Midi d'un Faune**, the boy yearns for a girl who eludes him. The unbearable intensity of both works is a result of their controlled movements. In the older ballet, this effect is created by its two dimensional appearance and by its use of slow motion. In Robbins' pas de deux it is created by the girl's contrived method of evasion and by both dancers' unwillingness to directly express their desires.

The boy wants the girl, but his inexperience makes him timid and insecure. Nonetheless, the intensity of his feeling induces him to make tentative advances.

The girl would like to reciprocate but she is more passive by nature, and timidity prevails over her attraction. We sense the two opposing forces within the protagonists, finding a different outcome in each.

Her withdrawal is subtle. The two have met ostensibly to rehearse a pas de deux, and she takes refuge in the choreography of their dance, pretending that this is the sole purpose of their tryst. Most of us can remember studying together as an excuse to meet a prospective lover. With each withdrawal, her beating heart hopes that he will again advance. Although she is too nervous and afraid of this new experience, it is clear that she wants him and does not know how to respond. Both are young, naive, shy and terrified. Despite their fear, they are in a rapture long forgotten by their elders.

The girl conceals her anxious delight at the lightest, most daring of kisses. As she turns her head stiffly away, we see a fleeting smile which has escaped the boy's notice. She appears frozen. Simply unable to handle the situation, she backs silently away, not moving her upper body. But her stiff position expresses sheer ecstasy. This is the only manner in which she can convey to the boy her true feelings, for she does not know what else to do. Both adolescents feel satisfied at the outcome of the adventure. Left alone, the boy stretches luxuriously. The curtain falls, and the spell is broken. We can become little again, our senses dulled by experience.

The suggestion of a mirror through which we see the dancers is a brilliant device. From the audience we get the impression that we are looking at the reflection of our past selves. The two dancers have perfect privacy in their closed world, the only people in existence.

They gaze at their reflections not only in a pretense of rehearsing properly, but also to avoid looking at each other and yet at the same time seeking indirect contact. In addition, they look for reassurance in the beauty of those reflections. When they think they are not being watched, they reveal to the mirror the fact that their newly matured, untested bodies are still a source of wonder to them. Though revelling in their newfound attractiveness, they have no confidence in it. In each, the self-admiration disappears abruptly when the new body is about to be tested on another person. The two are deeply insecure, utterly thrilled, and frightened out of their wits at the prospect of seeing themselves as objects to each other.

Youth is a painful and lonely time that we are eager to forget. But it is important that Robbins has preserved a moment of crystal perfection so we can remember and sympathize. And so we can recapture how it felt when the world was new.

I will now introduce a character from the ballet repertoire who has been much maligned over the years. No less a personage than Ulanova herself has told us that this was always her favourite role. Such an endorsement by itself ought to prompt a closer look. "Cinderella", she has said, "is the heart of goodness".

It is no easy task to isolate the one quality of simple sweetness and to express it without embellishment. Cinderella is not sparkling and witty like Aurora. She is not fragile and vulnerable like Giselle. She is not heroically determined like Juliet. She is the personification of something very basic which must exist in each of these characters, which indeed must exist in any character with whom we are to empathize, even as a tiny seed of goodness, for without this one quality we would find the character to be of little interest.

Cinderella is a personification of our potential for redemption, our ability to care about what someone else feels, our capacity for remorse and true humility. She knows no vanity, which as Sartre suggested is the mistake of viewing oneself as an object for another's eyes without fully recognizing that as an object one is not important. Cinderella knows that we are all subjects, not objects, and that we are all important, and when she considers another person's point of view she does not hold back and worry over what that person thinks of her. True love is not vulnerable, because it does not pause to consider its own welfare.

This is not to say that the rest of us do not love, but we have various imperfections in our complex personalities as we are concerned with our own welfare. When we see **Cinderella** we see that heart of goodness without embellishment. Seldom in our lives do we discard the trappings. Seldom do we bare our souls in abject and unguarded humility, without compromise. We shroud them in self flattery for our own protection, and with good reason. But it was when Moll Flanders confessed to every crime that she was given reprieve. And it is only when we cease searching for Moksha that we attain it.

Cinderella is the part of us that is not looking for a reprieve. When she dreams of dancing with the prince her thoughts alone satisfy her, though she is wistful for a moment because she would like to make a man happy someday. She never stops to consider whether or not she is worthy to marry a prince, and therefore while she is wide-eyed at her good fortune she can accept it with gratitude. She has neither high nor low self esteem. She does not reflect upon herself. She is simple and direct.

Cinderella's story is the most beloved of fairy tales because every girl or woman who has experienced hardship or misfortune would like her dreams to come true. You may notice that nobody ever identifies with the stepsisters. Everyone identifies with the meek heroine. But those who even fleetingly dream of inheriting the earth are not meek. Cinderella does not dwell upon her dreams. She is not a gold digger. She is surprised and grateful to her godmother. When she returns from the ball, she is not depressed at her glum prospects. She treasures her beautiful memories. She genuinely tries to fit her stepsister's foot into her own slipper, and when its mate falls out of her pocket her reaction is modest embarrassment, as if she has done something wrong in outshining others.

I can never fail to be moved by the loving gaze which follows and by the immediacy of the prince's response as he gathers his bride into his arms. That single movement comes straight from the heart which loves goodness, the heart which knows that you do not need even features, straight limbs, a bright mind or a great vision to be beautiful and to know the truth. With that movement comes the end to her suffering, and all the love she has been denied. But in a way, Cinderella has already been happy. She never categorized her wishes as needs. How her stepsisters must have envied her. I am tempted to think that perhaps she should have been left with her broom.

We like to reward on the basis of merit rather than need. I would say that we are, for the most part, barbaric. This is certainly a step up from a primitive penchant for punishing innocents, but if we were truly civilized we would understand what Socrates said to his wife before his death. She lamented, "They are killing an innocent man". He replied, "Would you be happier if I were guilty?" However, it is good that Cinderella enjoys her reward, which enables her to bring happiness to even more people than before. Any gifts to the stepsisters would have been piled on quicksand.

There is a religious message in Cinderella's true character. For what if the prize had been eternity? Those who are motivated by a desire for immortality shall be denied it, and anyone who complains "I wasn't trying for it, and yet still it was denied" obviously was in fact harbouring that motivation. The point is that we must give up hoping for it, assume we are unworthy and take what comes. Really.

Another of my favourite characters belongs to an obscure work with which many knowledgeable balletomanes have never been acquainted. It is my pleasure to introduce to you the young girl in Kenneth Macmillan's **Solitaire**, seemingly a pointless role in a minor ballet, but in fact one whose refreshing charm can cross the footlights straight into your heart.

Perhaps this is because most of us have been on the outside of some group or other in our lives and so we sympathize with her. Perhaps it is just because she has no idea that she should not project so far. I know of no other role in the ballet repertoire which departs from the social arrangement by which audience and performer are separated. In no other role is it appropriate to look directly at the audience members, person to person. This young girl can see us. We are brought into the diegesis of the ballet.

It is important when dancing the role not to be overtly perky and cute. The girl has Judy Garland's gift of being ingenuous and wide open to the world, to an impossible degree. There is no artifice, no vanity. She is simplicity itself. Her situation is funny but tinged with a sadness to which she is pathetically oblivious. She is as happy as can be when it seems that she might be accepted by other people. She is hurt momentarily at each rejection but returns every time, eternally hopeful, with the expectant optimism seen only in toddlers and dogs. After each blow the dear little soul comes back again, never learning, incapable of bias to the point of stupidity. And the characters onstage, as well as those in the audience, eventually abandon their resistance and come to love her because they wish they could be like that. And somewhere down deep inside they are, or they wouldn't wish it.

Solitaire is about the race war in America, and about every other civil war in which enemies have to interact on a daily basis. It is unreasonable to expect a person to take blow after blow without a hurt expression, without batting an eyelash. Each of us brings an accumulated past to every new situation. Our faces betray the fact that we expect to be hurt, and they trigger a defensive response in our enemies. We have survived by learning from what has already happened, and it is impossible for us to treat each experience as entirely new, to hold ourselves up for bombardment. David Hume noted that the process by which we surmise cause and effect is not a logical one; unfolding events are forever new. But we cannot fully understand that fact, however carefully we may have been taught to distinguish between an individual and a group. Only a created character on a stage can show us what might have been, impressing upon us why it is that we become biased —because we are afraid of being hurt.

The ballet I have saved for last is **Dances at a Gathering** because for me it carries a profound meaning. Although its choreography must have been carefully thought out, the effect is one of spontaneity. The movement seems to flow out of the emotions of the moment. Each character has a distinct personality and a distinct relationship to each of the others, and I always get the impression that feelings are being honestly expressed. I realize that this effect is achieved by means of artifice, but since that is entirely legitimate, on a higher level **Dances at a Gathering** is a very honest work.

When I first saw this ballet I wondered how it could possibly end. I was astonished at what happened. Jerome Robbins elevated these beautiful little creations by clarifying the meaning behind them. Each dancer seemed to be saying, "What a wonderful and holy thing it is to be a human being and to be able to express this miracle, a unique and precious person, for all the world to see". The reverence with which the man in green places his hand on the ground is a regard for the source of all nature and for the life which each person cherishes. After a pregnant silence, the women and men bow and courtesy with a rare dignity born of respect for each other as well as for themselves, a recognition of the wonder that is each other's being as well as their own.

The T'ang dynasty poet Wei T'ai wrote, "Poetry presents the thing in order to convey the feeling". In **Dances at a Gathering** Robbins has presented the thing itself with no explanation. And I feel rather curmudgeonly, trying to put it in words. Sir Francis Bacon said, "The best part of beauty is that which a picture cannot express", and I am doubly removed, trying to express the picture.

It is definitely time for me to stop.

THE BALLETS